SCIENCE Companions

Andrew Porter B.Sc.
In charge of Lower School Science,
Batley High School for Boys

Maria Wood B.Ed.
Formerly Assistant Science Teacher,
Batley High School for Boys

Trevor Wood B.Sc.
Head of Chemistry and Head of Sixth Form,
Batley High School for Boys

■ The Earth in Space
■ Earth & Atmosphere
■ Types and Uses of Materials
■ Human Influences
  on the Earth
■ Energy

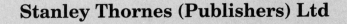

Stanley Thornes (Publishers) Ltd

First published in 1991 by:
Stanley Thornes (Publishers) Ltd
Old Station Drive
Leckhampton
CHELTENHAM GL53 0DN
England

British Library Cataloguing in Publication Data
Porter, Andrew
    Science companions.
    Book 1.
    1. Earth sciences
    I. Title II. Wood, Maria III. Wood, Trevor
    550

ISBN 0 7487 0550 3

Design and illustrations by Cauldron Design Studio,
Berwickshire
Typeset by Word Power, Berwickshire

Printed and bound in Singapore

Acknowledgements

The authors wish to acknowledge the
dedication and expertise of the staff of Stanley
Thornes Publishers. We would like to thank all
those involved for their expert guidance and
high standards of production. Special thanks to
Ruth Holmes, Jennifer Johnson and Cauldron
Design Studio.

The authors and publishers are grateful to the
following for permission to reproduce
photographs:
p.2 top right NASA/Science Photo Library, p.2
centre Novosti/Science Photo Library, p.5 x 2
NASA/Science Photo Library, p.10 Julian
Baum/Science Photo Library, p.14 J. Allan
Cash, p.15 left Vivien Fifield, p.15 right Ann
Ronan, p.17 top Robin Scagell/Science Photo
Library, p.17 bottom David Parker/Science
Photo Library, p.24 Popperfoto, p.25 David
Hoadley/Frank Lane Picture Agency, p.29 Zefa,
p.30 Photri/Barnaby's Picture Library, p.31
Ronald Sheridan Photo Library, p.32
GeoScience Features, p.34 top x 2 Alain Le
Garsmeur/Impact, p.34 bottom left Jesco Von
Puttkamer/Hutchison Library, p.34 bottom
right GeoScience Features, p.35 top left
GeoScience Features, p.35 top right M.J.
Thomas/Celtic Picture Library, p.35 bottom
J.G. Fuller/Hutchison Library, p.39 top J. Allan
Cash, p.39 bottom Dr Jeremy Burgess/Science
Photo Library, p.43 top left Trevor Hill, p.43
bottom left Ronald Sheridan, p.43 top right
Shell UK, p.46 left Biophotos, p.46 right Trevor
Hill, p.49 Heinz, p.50 x 3 Trevor Hill, p.51 x 2
Trevor Wood, p.54 left Steve McCutcheon/
Frank Lane Picture Agency, p.54 middle, right
J. Allan Cash, p.55 top left J. Allan Cash, p.55
top centre Alan Felix/Barnaby's Picture
Library, p.55 top right W.J.V Puttkamer, p.55
centre x 2 Shell UK, p.55 bottom David T.
Grewcock/Frank Lane Picture Agency, p.62 top
right V. Miles/Environment Picture Library,
p.62 left Foote/Greenpeace, p. 62 right Trevor
Hill, p.66 A.R. Hamblin/Frank Lane Picture
Agency, p.71 top right Dr Booth/GeoScience
Features, p.71 left Desmond Dugan/Frank
Lane Picture Agency, p.71 right NASA/Science
Photo Library, p.73 Dr Jeremy Burgess/Science
Photo Library, p.78 x 2 Trevor Hill, p.79 Chris
Beetles Ltd, p.82 top Ann Ronan, p.82 bottom
Zefa, p.83 top Heilman/Zefa, p.83 bottom
Simon Fraser/Science Photo Library, p.85 Zefa.

We are grateful to the following for permission
to reproduce artwork and text: p.8 *Daily
Telegraph*, p.18 *Daily Telegraph*, p.40 Patons,
p.40 Sirdar PLC, p.45 *Guardian*, p.64
Guardian, p.85 Manx Electricity Authority,
p.86 McVities, p.88 Reproduced by permission
of Kellog Company of Great Britain Limited,
p.88 Mars, p.88 Tilda Rice.

Contents

Contents of *Science Companions Book 2*

Contents of *Science Companions Book 3*

Introduction

Science Companions offer an activity-based science course covering levels 3–5 of the National Curriculum. There are three books in all, addressing the Programmes of Study for Key Stage 3 (years 7–9).

Each book is organised into self-contained Themes which relate to the attainment targets of the National Curriculum. Each Theme is presented as double page spreads – packed with lively, original science.

Full colour spreads provide factual information and explanations. These spreads include work on the nature of science.

Information is balanced with Activities which develop the science from the preceding two pages through 'Try it Yourself' practical activities, questions, puzzles and suggestions for further research. In many cases, pupils will need to work on a copy of the Activity pages alongside the book. This may be a copy that the pupil has made or alternatively, a photocopy. The practical activities are, in most cases, simple home-based explorations of science. Indeed, these books will find a use at home as well as in the classroom.

The two related books which complement this one each follow an identical format to complete the National Curriculum coverage. Separate Answer Books are available from the Publisher.

Limited resources

Everything we use comes from the planet we live on. Although it may seem that resources such as coal or iron ore will last forever, we know that in the end they are limited. Some resources, e.g. oil, may begin to run out in your lifetime. Others, e.g. uranium, will last a lot longer.

People have come to appreciate the limited resources of our Earth partly by seeing the planet from space. They saw how beautiful the planet is, and realised that it is up to everyone to make the best use of it.

Orbiting Earth

To see the Earth from space, people had to build rockets which would travel fast enough to escape from the Earth. At a certain height above the Earth, a rocket (or anything carried by it) will go round the planet without crashing to the ground, as long as it travels fast enough. We say it is **orbiting** the Earth.

◄
The first object to orbit the Earth was a radiotransmitter called *Sputnik 1* on 4 October 1957. Here it is opened up to show the parts inside. In orbit it was a sphere.

►
The first human to orbit the Earth was Yuri Gagarin on 12 April 1961. He made one revolution in a flight lasting 108 minutes.

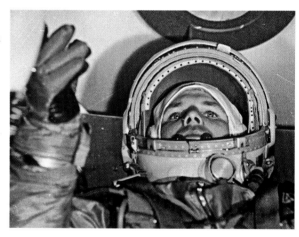

Moon landings

The Moon is easy to see with the naked eye. It is large (nearly 3500 km across, about one-quarter the diameter of Earth), and like *Sputnik 1* it orbits the Earth. Both *Sputnik 1* and the Moon are called **satellites** – they are objects that orbit a planet.

By 1969, space travel had advanced enough to land on the Moon. Neil Armstrong was the first person to step on the Moon, followed by his partner Edwin 'Buzz' Aldrin. The astronauts found it easy to move about on the Moon because they only weighed one-sixth of their Earth weight. Someone weighing 60 kg on the Earth will only weigh 10 kg on the Moon. This is because **gravity** on the Moon is weaker than that on Earth. The Moon exerts a smaller force on things than the Earth does. The astronauts found it easier to bounce around (or Moon-hop) rather than try to walk.

The phases of the Moon

The Moon orbits the Earth and the Earth orbits the Sun. Both the Earth and the Moon are lit by the rays of the Sun. The Moon does not shine by itself. It reflects the light from the Sun. When we look at the Moon, different sides of it are lit up depending on where the Sun, Moon and Earth are.

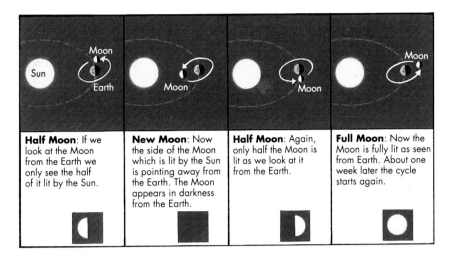

Half Moon: If we look at the Moon from the Earth we only see the half of it lit by the Sun.

New Moon: Now the side of the Moon which is lit by the Sun is pointing away from the Earth. The Moon appears in darkness from the Earth.

Half Moon: Again, only half the Moon is lit as we look at it from the Earth.

Full Moon: Now the Moon is fully lit as seen from Earth. About one week later the cycle starts again.

Lunar eclipse

The Moon takes about four weeks to orbit the Earth once. Sometimes, when the Earth is between the Sun and the Moon, it casts a shadow over the Moon. The Moon disappears from sight for a short time. This is called a **lunar eclipse**. It does not happen every time there is a full Moon because the Sun, Earth and Moon are not always in a straight line.

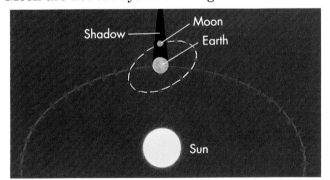

Solar eclipse

In a similar way, the Moon can come between the Sun and the Earth. This results in the more spectacular **solar eclipse**. The light from the Sun is blocked out by the Moon and the Earth (or part of it) is cast in darkness. The next solar eclipse in the UK will happen in 1999 and will be seen from south-west England.

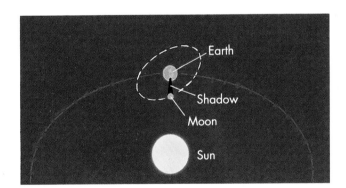

QUESTIONS

1. Why are some resources such as oil going to run out?

2. What was the first satellite launched into space?

3. Who was the first person on the Moon? Find out what his first words were.

4. Why do astronauts on the Moon wear protective clothing and face masks? (See the photograph on page 5.)

5. Draw diagrams to show what the Moon will look like from the Earth
   a) between half Moon and full Moon
   b) between half Moon and new Moon.

6. Approximately how many times does the Moon go round the Earth in one year?

7. Why is there not a total eclipse of the Sun every four weeks?

1. Imagine you are Yuri Gagarin, just about to launch into space for the first time, or Neil Armstrong, about to set foot on the Moon. Write a story showing how you feel. What do you want to know before setting out?

2. Answer the questions below. On your own copy, complete the voyage to the Moon using your answers. The last letter of each answer makes the first letter of the next answer.

   1. The planet our journey starts from.
   2. The movement that astronauts make on the Moon.
   3. The different shapes of the Moon as seen from the Earth.
   4. Something that orbits the Earth.
   5. What we use to observe the sky.
   6. This lights up the Earth and the Moon.
   7. The name we give to the Moon when only the dark side can be seen from Earth.
   8. There is none of this on the Moon.
   9. What we need to get to the Moon.

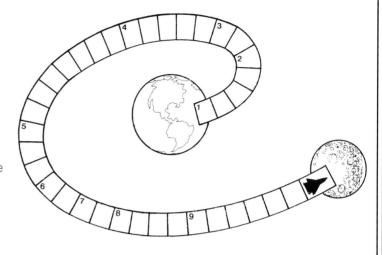

Voyage to the Moon

3. Explain in your own words what is meant by
   a) a lunar eclipse
   b) a solar eclipse.

4. Look at these pictures of the space shuttle. They are not in the right order. Write out the letters of the pictures in the correct order.

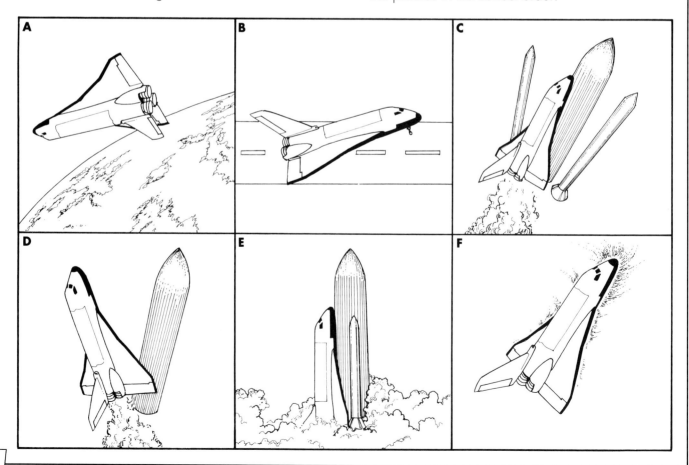

1. a) How many people have walked on the Moon?
   b) When was the last Apollo mission to the Moon?
   c) Which Apollo mission did not make it to the Moon? Why?

Edwin Aldrin walking on the Moon, July 1969

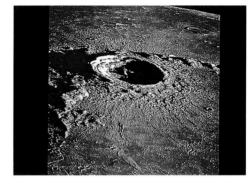

2. The surface of the Moon is covered in craters.
   a) How were these craters made?
   b) Why have they lasted so long when the craters on Earth have mostly disappeared?

Try it yourself

1. *Moonwatch*

   Keep a diary over several weeks, whenever the sky is clear enough at night to see the Moon. Make a grid of squares like the one opposite. Draw in the shape of the Moon each day you can see it, and add the date. Look for the repeating pattern.

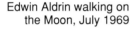

1 December	4 December			
🌙	🌙			

2. *A lunar landscape model*

   YOU WILL NEED THESE...

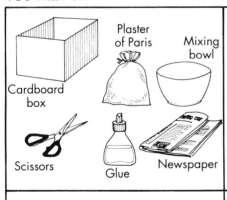

Plaster of Paris   Mixing bowl

Cardboard box

Scissors   Glue   Newspaper

Mark the box with diagonal lines on two opposite sides. Cut away the sides to leave a corner piece.

Cut some strips about 1 cm wide using the remaining cardboard.

Bend them into circles and glue together.

Stick down the circles with strips of newspaper.

Build up the strips to make the circles into craters.

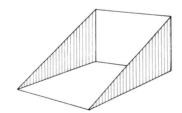

Mix Plaster of Paris according to the instructions.

IMPORTANT
If you need to use the bowl again, wash it out before the plaster sets.

Spread the plaster over the base of the model.

Make peaks in the plaster before it sets.

Leave to set and paint with poster paints.

☐ ☐ ☐ Information ☐ ☐ ☐

Here are the nine planets that orbit the Sun. Together with the asteroids and comets, they make up the **Solar System**. The planet sizes are shown to scale, but they are not at the right distances apart. To show these distances in proportion to the sizes drawn here the book would need to be over 2 kilometres wide!

The Sun is not drawn to scale. It is far bigger than all the planets put together and would be about 60 cm across on the same scale.

The length of day is the time it takes for each planet to spin round once, measured in Earth time. The length of year is the time taken to go round the Sun once, measured in Earth time.

Mercury
$\frac{1}{3}$ the size of Earth
6 months to spin round once
3 months to go round the Sun
No satellites
Temperature 400 °C to –200 °C
Rocky surface

Earth
24 hours to spin round once
12 months to go round the Sun
1 satellite
Temperature 20 °C
Rocky surface with water

Mariner
Galileo
Viking
Asteroid belt

Venus
Slightly smaller than Earth
4 months to spin round once
7 months to go round Sun
No satellites
Temperature 480 °C
Rocky surface under thick clouds

Mars
$\frac{1}{4}$ the size of Earth
24 hours to spin round once
2 years to go round Sun
2 satellites
Temperature –60 °C
Rocky surface

Jupiter
11 times larger than Earth
10 hours to spin round once
12 years to go round Sun
16 satellites
Temperature –120 °C
Surface of gases with liquid hydrogen and helium below

QUESTIONS

1. Which planets have rings?
2. Which planets are the 'gas giants'?
3. Why do the planets get colder from Venus to Pluto?
4. Why does Pluto have the longest year?
5. Why do you think we are unsure about the figures for Pluto?
6. What makes Earth different from all other planets?
7. What planets did *Voyager 2* visit?
8. Which planet has
   a) the longest
   b) the shortest day?

Saturn
9 times larger than Earth
10.6 hours to spin round once
29 years to go round Sun
17 satellites
Temperature −180 °C
Surface like Jupiter's

Voyager1

Voyager2

Uranus
4 times larger than Earth
16 hours to spin round once
84 years to go round Sun
15 satellites
Temperature −220 C
Surface like Jupiter's

Neptune
3.5 times larger than Earth
17 hours to spin round once
164 years to go round Sun
2 satellites
Temperature −230 °C
Surface like Jupiter's

Pluto
$\frac{1}{4}$? the size of Earth
7 days to spin round once
247 years to orbit the Sun
1 satellite
Temperature −230 °C(?)
Surface of ice and rocks

MARCH NIGHT SKY ★ ★ ★ ★ ★ ★

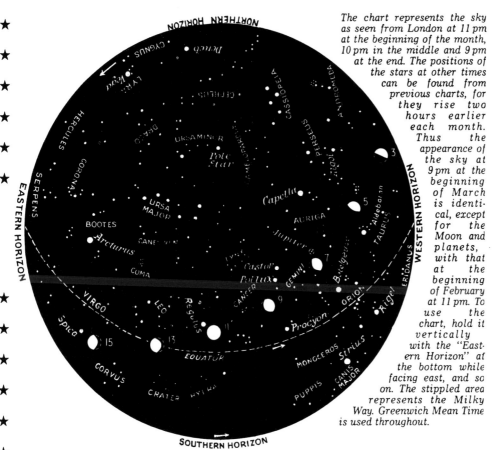

The chart represents the sky as seen from London at 11 pm at the beginning of the month, 10 pm in the middle and 9 pm at the end. The positions of the stars at other times can be found from previous charts, for they rise two hours earlier each month. Thus the appearance of the sky at 9 pm at the beginning of March is identical, except for the Moon and planets, with that at the beginning of February at 11 pm. To use the chart, hold it vertically with the "Eastern Horizon" at the bottom while facing east, and so on. The stippled area represents the Milky Way. Greenwich Mean Time is used throughout.

MERCURY comes into superior conjunction on the 20th, when it will be 125 million miles from the Earth on the far side of the Sun. It does not elongate sufficiently from the Sun to be visible this month.

VENUS rises in the south-east at 4.45 am early in the month and half an hour earlier at the end. In mid-March it is 10 deg high at 5.45 am, half an hour before sunrise.

At 5.30 am on the 23rd Venus will be 10 deg high and above the decrescent Moon, brilliant at magnitude − 4.4.

Venus reaches greatest elongation on the 30th, when it will be 63 million miles from the Earth and 46 deg west of the Sun.

MARS will be visible to the right of Venus throughout the month, but at magnitude only 1.1 it is fainter than several stars in the sky at the time. It is identifiable by its reddish tint and its steady light.

At 5 am on the 22nd Mars will be 5 deg high and to the left of the decrescent Moon.

JUPITER is very high, due south, as soon as the sky is really dark, about 7 pm at the beginning of the month, and sets in the north-west at 3 am. In the middle of March when the Sun sets at 6 pm the planet will already be in the south-western sky as twilight turns to darkness, very bright at magnitude − 2.3.

On the evening of the 4th Jupiter will be seen to the left of the First Quarter Moon and on the 5th it will be well to the right.

SATURN is visible low in the south-east about half an hour before sunrise, and at the end of the first week in March it is 10 deg high at 6 am. At the end of the month it rises two and a half hours before the Sun.

At the beginning of March Saturn will be seen fairly close to the right of Venus and Mars, but by the end it will have been left far behind.

Saturn will be to the left of the decrescent Moon on the morning of the 21st.

---

1. Articles like this one appear in the *Daily Telegraph* at the end of each month. They give details of what will be seen in the night sky for the month ahead. Look out for articles similar to this one in newspapers. Read this one and then answer the questions below.

   a) Which planets apart from the Earth are mentioned in the article?

   b) Which will be visible in the sky during March?

   c) How far away will Mercury be on 20 March?

   d) Why does Mars have a 'reddish tint'?

   e) On what day in March was there a full Moon?

2. The planet Pluto is shrouded in mystery. Nobody has seen pictures of its surface. Write a story telling how you think the surface of Pluto might look and make a drawing. How could a human survive on Pluto?

3. Read this newspaper article and answer the questions which follow.

Sailing to Mars

There are plans to organise a race to the planet Mars. The race is due to coincide with the 500th anniversary of Christopher Columbus's voyage to America in 1492.

Like Columbus, the entries in the Mars race will not have access to engine power. They will have to sail to Mars. This may sound impossible, since there are no winds as we know them in space. However, the Sun gives out a stream of small particles in all directions. These make up the **solar wind**.

On Earth, this solar wind is responsible for the Northern Lights or Aurora Borealis. The solar wind is capable of propelling a spacecraft from Earth orbit to Mars, as long as the sail is large enough.

Entries are proposed from the USA, Canada, China and Japan. The spacecraft will be put into orbit around the Earth by rocket, but then they are on their own. The prize will go to the craft that gets to within 16 000 km of Mars.

The sails need to be very large indeed. One entry, called the *Nina*, has sails which fold out to the size of four Wembley Stadiums.

a) Why is the race planned for 1992?
b) What causes the solar wind?
c) What happens when the solar wind hits the Earth?
d) Why would it not be possible to sail to Venus?
e) Why do the sails need to fold away when the craft are launched?
f) Design your own space sailing ship. Remember it must have sails that can be folded away for launching.

4. a) On your own copy, fill in the names of the missing planets.
b) Which two planets are missing from this list?

Try it yourself

1. A scale model of the Solar System
You will need a lot of space for this. It is best done outside or along a long corridor. You may still run out of room!
The planets are represented by circles cut out of card and coloured in. You could stick them on wooden spikes to drive them into the ground, or pin them on the walls of a corridor.
The Sun may be too large to cut out. It will have to be 280 cm in diameter (across).
For the planets, cut out small circles. The circles should have the diameters given below.

Name	Diameter	Distance from the Sun
Mercury	1 cm	12.5 cm
Venus	3 cm	21 cm
Earth	3 cm	30 cm
Mars	2 cm	45 cm
Jupiter	29 cm	155 cm
Saturn	24 cm	285 cm
Uranus	12 cm	570 cm
Neptune	10 cm	900 cm
Pluto	1 cm	1200 cm

The scale of the planet sizes is not the same as the scale of their distances. The planets would have to be 1000 times further away if both scales were the same.
Here is something else to think about. The *Voyager* probes set off from Earth and made their way to most of the outer planets. On this scale, they would be smaller than a piece of dust! On this scale Pluto looks far away, but the nearest star to the Sun would be much further – over 160 km away!

Science Companions 1 © A Porter, M Wood, T Wood and Stanley Thornes (Publishers) Ltd, 1991

❑ ❑ ❑ The stars in the sky ❑ ❑ ❑

On a clear night, anyone with good eyesight can see thousands of stars. In fact, there are many more stars. The others are too faint or too far away to be seen from Earth without using a telescope or binoculars.

The brightest star in the sky is also the nearest and we know it as the Sun. It is so bright to us on Earth that during the day when it appears in the sky, the Sun outshines all other stars and we cannot see them. Only when the Sun has set at night can we observe the other, more distant stars.

Compared with other stars, the Sun is of average size and brightness. There are many larger stars like Betelgeuse, which is over 100 times larger than our Sun. There are many stars that would outshine the Sun if they were closer – Rigel is 50 000 times brighter.

Sunspots are areas of the Sun that are less hot than the rest of the surface. These are the spots you can see on the surface of the Sun.

❑ ❑ ❑ ❑ ❑ ❑ ❑ How stars shine ❑ ❑ ❑ ❑ ❑ ❑ ❑

All stars give out a large amount of heat, light and other kinds of energy. In order to do this they use a fuel. The most common material in the universe is hydrogen. Stars use hydrogen as a fuel. They cannot burn hydrogen in the way that we can burn it, because there is no air around them. They burn it at much higher temperatures than we do. Stars use hydrogen as a **nuclear fuel**.

The stars at night appear to twinkle. This has nothing to do with the way they shine. The twinkling is an illusion caused by the Earth's atmosphere.

The life story of our Sun

There is an attraction between all objects which we call **gravity**. We only notice gravity when the objects are very big, like the Sun or the Earth. It is this attraction that made it possible for the Sun to form.

1. Gas and dust had been formed from other exploding stars. It took over a million years for the gas and dust to pull together.

2. The centre of the cloud began to get hot as nuclear reactions started. Planets began to form from the swirling gas and dust that were left orbiting the centre.

3. Today the Sun shines brightly. The planets have formed. There is life on Earth. The Sun is nearing the half-way point in its life. It is 4.5 billion years old.

4. The Sun's nuclear fuel will begin to run out and the gravity holding the star together will weaken. The Sun will expand and swallow up the Earth.

5. The Sun will explode. It will throw unused hydrogen into space.

6. The core of the Sun will collapse to a fraction of the size it is today. A star at this stage is known as a **white dwarf**.

7. Eventually this white dwarf will cool down and stop giving out heat or light. The cold black remains are called a **black dwarf**.

QUESTIONS

1. What are sunspots?

2. Why can we not see stars other than the Sun during the day?

3. What fuels do stars use? Why do they use it?

4. Why do stars twinkle?

5. Name a star that is larger than the Sun. Which star is brighter?

6. What will eventually happen to the Earth at the end of its life?

7. What will the Sun eventually become?

WARNING: Never look at the Sun. It is so bright that the light will damage your eyes.

1. Space crossword

Fill in the grid on your own copy.

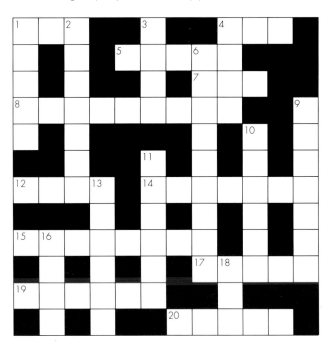

Across

1. The nearest star to Earth.
4. Short for Greenwich Mean Time.
5. This means belonging to the Moon.
7. The colour of the planet Mars.
8. The science of the stars and planets.
12. We must protect these when studying the Sun.
14. The nearest planet to the Sun.
15. The commonest gas in the universe.
17. These make the atmosphere of planets.
19. The planet that takes 84 years to go round the Sun.
20. The living planet.

Down

1. This means belonging to the Sun.
2. The last planet that *Voyager 2* visited.
3. Another word for spin.
4. The colour of Moon rock.
6. The surname of the first man on the Moon.
9. The biggest on Earth is called the Grand, but there are bigger ones on Mars.
10. The top layers of the inner planets.
11. Pictures sent back by probes.
13. One of the four seasons.
16. The forename of the first man to orbit the Earth.
18. This is only found on the planet Earth.

Try it yourself

1. How to find south

If you have a watch with hands (not a digital watch) and you know where the Sun is in the sky, you can work out the direction of the South Pole. Point the hour hand towards the Sun. South is in the direction half-way between the hour hand and the 12. Before noon, south is to the left of the 12, and in the afternoon it is to the right.

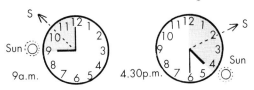

On your own copy, complete these diagrams to answer the questions.

a) What is the position of the Sun?

b) Draw an arrow on the watches to show the direction of south.

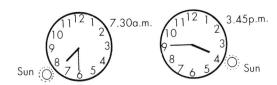

c) What would the position of the Sun be at noon?

d) This only works when the watch is set to Greenwich Mean Time. How could you use the method in summer when the clocks are put forward?

2. Make a sundial

Trace the pattern opposite on to card. Cut out the triangle and glue it on to the sundial along line A. The triangle must stick up straight. The base of the sundial must be flat and the arrow on the base must point south.

Helpful hints

- Glue the base to a piece of wood for extra support.
- The sundial will be an hour out if you are doing this in the summertime. The sundial works in Greenwich Mean Time. If the clocks have been put forward, you need to adjust the time.

Science Companions 1 © A Porter, M Wood, T Wood and Stanley Thornes (Publishers) Ltd, 1991

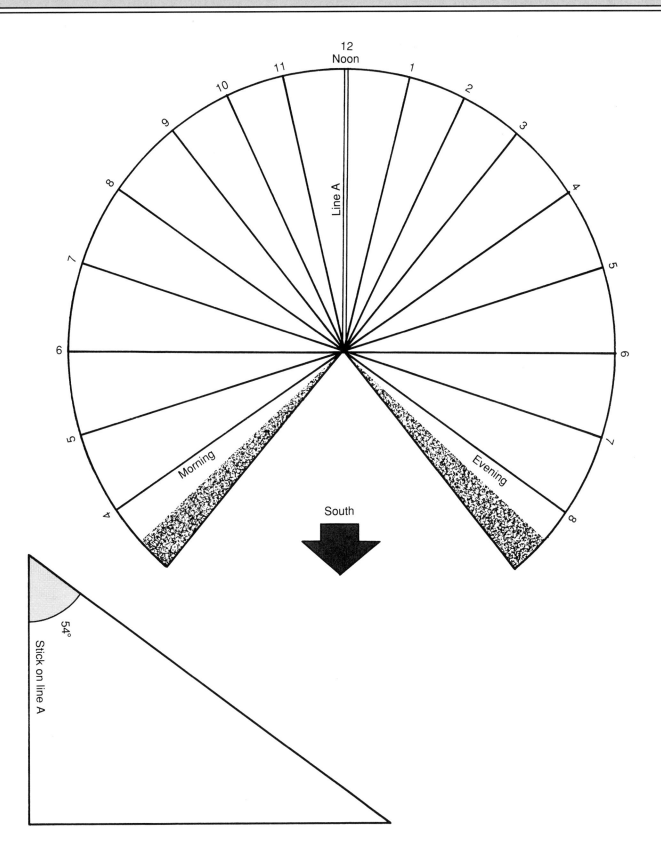

- If you have difficulty in finding south, then follow the instructions in activity 1.
- The angle of the triangle has to be set to the latitude where you live. You can usually find this on a map. The triangle here is set to 54° which is right for the middle of the UK. The angle varies between 50° for south Cornwall and 59° for north Scotland.
- Of course, the sundial will only work if the Sun is bright enough to cast a shadow!

cience Companions 1 © A Porter, M Wood, T Wood and Stanley Thornes (Publishers) Ltd, 1991

Our views of the universe

For thousands of years people have watched the skies. When we trace the path of the Sun across the sky, we notice several patterns. The Sun rises in the east and sets in the west every day. In summer, the Sun is higher in the sky than in winter. It takes more time to move from sunrise to sunset, so the days are longer in summer. In winter the days are shorter.

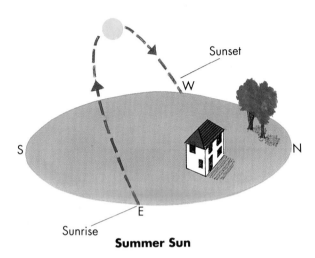

Summer Sun

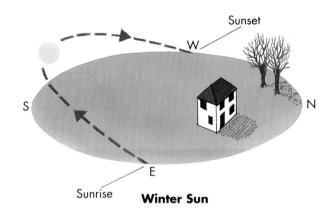

Winter Sun

These patterns are so obvious that people were able to predict them back in the Stone Age. It seems likely that places like Stonehenge were built so that every year, at midsummer, the Sun would rise over a particular stone and shine into the stone circle.

It is easy for us to think that the Earth is standing still and the Sun goes round the Earth. This idea, however, does not explain all the observations we can make from Earth. For example, how do we explain why the Sun is higher in the sky in summer? (For the answer to this question see the Activities section on the next pages.)

Another observation that cannot be explained this way is that planets make curved tracks in the sky at night. They do not move in straight lines like the Sun or the Moon. People have noticed for a long time that they loop back on themselves.

The story of how we now explain the universe can be traced back to the ancient Greeks. They believed that the Earth was at the centre of everything. The Moon, Sun, planets and stars travelled around the Earth. This remained the official explanation for many centuries.

Stonehenge

Nicolaus Copernicus (1473–1543) was a Polish man who was asked by the Catholic Church to see how they could improve their calendar. He realised that there must be a simple explanation of the paths of the planets. He put the Sun at the centre of the universe. The planets, including Earth, went around the Sun. He knew his ideas went against the teachings of the Catholic Church at the time.

They had said that the ancient Greeks were right. Copernicus did not publish his ideas until the last year of his life.

Johannes Kepler (1571–1630) later worked out the orbits of the planets in more detail. This simplified version of the Solar System exactly fitted what we see from Earth.

The main character to challenge the Catholic Church's ideas was Galileo Galilei (1564–1642). He had built the most powerful telescope of his time. It could magnify things to about 30 times their real size. This meant that he could see the planet Jupiter. Galileo noted that the planet had four moons going around it. From this observation it was clear that the Earth could not be the centre of everything, because the centre for these moons was Jupiter. Since everyone who cared to look through his telescope could see this for themselves, Galileo thought that would be the end of the matter.

Copernicus

Galileo

However, the Catholic Church was facing rebellion from many sides at the time. The Protestant Church had recently formed in many countries. In England, Henry VIII had rebelled against the Catholic Church after a row with the Pope. The Catholic Church was in no mood to have its authority challenged. Galileo was threatened with torture. He signed a document saying that he did not believe the Sun was the centre of the universe.

Galileo died in the same year that Isaac Newton was born in England. It was Newton who was to work out, scientifically, the orbits of the planets using the laws of gravity. It was through his laws that we could send people to the Moon and probes deep into space.

QUESTIONS

1. Why are the days longer in summer than in winter?
2. Who came up with the idea of putting the Sun at the centre of the universe? Is this idea still believed?
3. What allowed Galileo to see the moons around Jupiter? Why was this discovery important?
4. Why did Galileo have difficulty persuading others that the Earth was not the centre of everything?
5. How old was Galileo when he died?
6. Why was Isaac Newton important to space travel today?

Isaac Newton

1. Look out for these groups of stars in the sky at night. A group of stars is called a **constellation**. The constellations look as if they are fixed in the sky. In fact, they will look that way for the rest of your life. However, they do change over a long period of time, because the stars are moving in different directions.

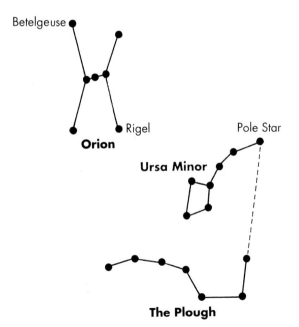

Betelgeuse

Rigel

Orion

Pole Star

Ursa Minor

The Plough

Try to spot the constellations in the picture at the top of this page.

2. Rearrange these letters to name things you can see in the night sky with the naked eye.

EVUNS   NOORI   MOSCET   KYLIM YAW
PRETIJU   GHOSTION RATS   CALLITONSTONE
GLUEEBEETS   ARLUN CIPEELS
RENTHORN GLITHS

Try it yourself

1. The Earth goes round the Sun at an angle. It spins on its axis at an angle of 23.5° to the vertical.

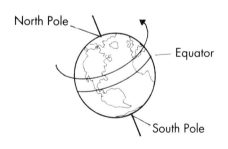

North Pole

Equator

South Pole

It is because of this angle that our day lengths and seasons change. To see this you can make a simple model of the Sun and the Earth. You will need a lamp without the shade, a block of wood, a large nail and an old tennis ball or something similar.

Carefully push the nail through the ball. Now hammer the nail into the block of wood at an angle. It does not have to be exact but if you use a protractor you can get close to 23.5°.

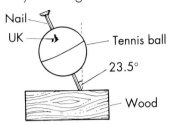

You could mark the position of the UK on the ball. It is roughly half-way between the North Pole and the Equator. To mark it accurately, look at a globe. Now place the ball with the North Pole pointing towards the lamp, which will play the part of the Sun. As the Earth spins around its axis (the nail) you can see that the UK spends more time in the light of the Sun and less time in shadow. The day is longer than the night. This is what happens in summer. Use a little imagination and pretend you are standing on the ball at the position of the UK in daytime. The Sun would be high in the sky. It shines down on the UK directly, warming it up quickly.

Lamp

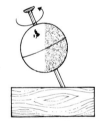

Summer: UK spends more time in daylight.

Now move the ball on its stand to the other side of the lamp. The North Pole should now be facing away from the Sun. We are now in winter. Turning the ball on the nail should show you that the nights are longer than the days and the Sun only strikes the Earth at a shallow angle. It does not get high in the sky and does not warm the UK as much as it does in summer.

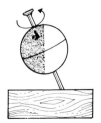

Winter: UK spends more time in shadow (night).

Lamp

a) What is the angle of the Earth's axis?
b) Why is the Sun hotter in the summer than in the winter?
c) What are the other two seasons, apart from summer and winter?
d) Where would the Earth (or tennis ball) be on your model during these two seasons?
e) The middle days of these two seasons are called the **equinoxes**. What happens to the length of day and night at the equinoxes?

2. You can easily take photographs of the night sky if you have a camera that allows you to keep the shutter open for a long time. Photographs turn out best on moonless nights and away from streetlights, but you can always experiment under different conditions. One thing you do need is a cloudless night. The camera has to remain very still as you take the photograph. You might be able to prop it up at an angle, or you may have a camera tripod. Try leaving the shutter open for different times, say 5 minutes, then 10, 15, and so on. In that time the Earth will have turned slightly. Your photograph of the stars will appear blurred. The results can be quite interesting.

If you point the camera towards the Pole Star you will get this result. Try to explain it.

Science Companions 1 © A Porter, M Wood, T Wood and Stanley Thornes (Publishers) Ltd, 1991

The weather

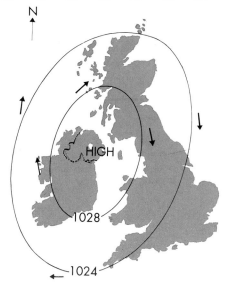

There are about 80 kilometres of air above us. All this air has a weight which presses down on us. We call this weight **air pressure**. We do not notice the air pressing down on us because it has always been there so we are used to it.

Air pressure is measured in **millibars** (mb) and has an average value of 1016 millibars at sea level. When the air pressure value is greater than this we say the pressure is high. An area of high pressure is called an **anticyclone**. An area of low pressure is called a **depression**.

Weather forecasters use maps which show high or low pressure areas. Lines are drawn on these maps joining places with the same air pressure. These lines are called **isobars**.

When we have an anticyclone over the UK the weather is calm. Winds are light and generally blow clockwise, slightly away from the centre of the anticyclone. In summer this gives cool, misty mornings followed by hot, clear, sunny afternoons. In the winter, mornings can be cold, frosty and foggy, followed by cold, clear, sunny afternoons.

Most of the winds over the UK blow from the south-west to the north-east. These are called the **prevailing winds**. This means that most of the weather blows in from the Atlantic Ocean. Areas of high and low pressure usually approach from the south-west and move to the north-east, as Low R does below.

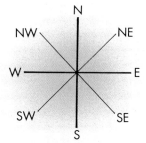

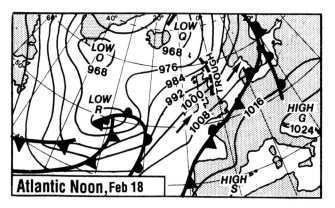

Atlantic Noon, Feb 18

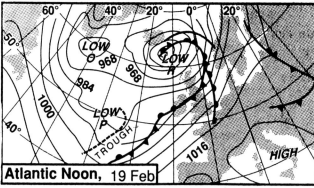

Atlantic Noon, 19 Feb

Depressions are usually about 1000 km across and consist of huge swirls of wind, cloud and rain. The spinning of the Earth causes the air to swirl. **Weather fronts** come with depressions. These are narrow bands of rain. They are formed because cold air is more dense than warm air. If cold air meets warm air, the cold air can force its way underneath the warm air, making the warm air rise. As the warm air rises it cools. The cooling condenses the water vapour in the air to form clouds and then rain. This is happening in the three fronts associated with Low R on the weather charts above.

Type of front	The weather we can expect
Cold front	Heavy rain, hail, even thunder
Warm front	Drizzly rain at the leading edge of the warm air
Occluded front	The warm front is followed straight away by the cold front and all the warm air has been lifted off the ground. Drizzly rain followed by heavy rain, with hail and thunder

In a depression the winds blow in an anticlockwise direction and usually slightly towards the centre of the depression, following the isobars.

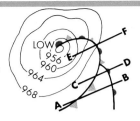

A depression showing typical isobars and weather fronts

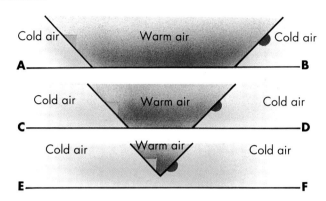

The cold and warm air across the lines A–B, C–D and E–F in the depression

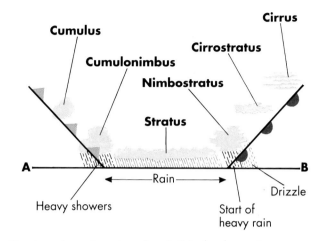

Clouds and weather along line A–B in the depression

Weather forecasting

The weather forecasts for the UK are prepared using a powerful computer at the Meteorological Office at Bracknell in Berkshire. Over a million separate pieces of information are gathered from satellites, radar stations, weather ships, aircraft and instruments carried by rockets and balloons. The forecasts are vital for the RAF and civil airlines. They are very accurate for weather above a height of 15 km. The television, radio and newspaper forecast is interpreted from the main data. The forecast is not so accurate near the ground because the Earth's surface affects the lower layers in the atmosphere.

Television weather is presented with the minimum of scientific explanation so it is easy to understand. To help, a range of symbols has been created. The recent introduction of computer graphics means that these basic symbols can now be made to move and present an even more realistic effect.

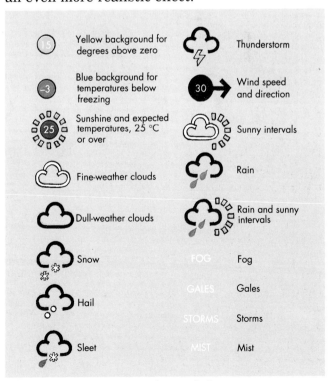

TV weather symbols

QUESTIONS

1. In which direction do winds blow round an anticyclone?

2. What weather is expected at a cold front?

3. What is the prevailing wind direction for the United Kingdom?

4. Why is the weather forecast more accurate above 15 km?

5. What is an isobar?

6. What type of cloud is associated with showers?

1. The weather can have a serious effect on the safety of our roads. In poor weather roads can be very dangerous.

   a) Suggest some sensible precautions a car driver should take in fog.

   b) Why does a car take a longer distance to stop on a wet road than on a dry road?

   c) Why are front-wheel drive cars generally better in snow than rear-wheel drive ones?

   d) Why is it necessary to try the brakes of a car after driving through a flood or ford?

   e) Why are high-sided vehicles often banned from bridges in windy weather?

2. Study the weather map opposite, then answer the questions which follow.

   a) Write down the letters **A** to **G**. Beside each letter draw the weather symbol which would be used by the television weather forecaster to show the weather people could expect there.

   b) What sort of weather fronts are shown on the map?

   c) Look at the isobars and their pressures. Explain why the winds are blowing in the directions shown.

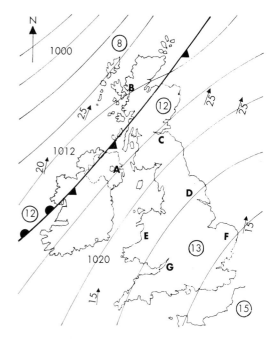

Key

A Belfast
B Kyle of Lochalsh
C Edinburgh
D Leeds
E Aberystwyth
F Norwich
G Bristol

3. Match the clothes to the weather symbols. Write down the letters A to E and beside each letter write the number of the best clothes for that weather.

4. Study carefully these weather figures for Belfast and London between 11 and 17 February 1990. Then answer the questions which follow.

   a) What was the total rainfall in millimetres for the week in Belfast?

   b) What was the total rainfall in millimetres for the week in London?

Belfast							
Date	11	12	13	14	15	16	17
Rain (mm)	2.0	3.2	3.2	1.3	1.5	0	0.5
Max. temperature (°C)	7	3	6	5	6	7	8
Sunshine (hours)	0	2.8	0.4	0	7.5	7.4	1.6
London							
Date	11	12	13	14	15	16	17
Rain (mm)	4.0	1.3	3.5	1.0	6.0	0	2.0
Max. temperature (°C)	9	9	10	8	9	10	12
Sunshine (hours)	0.1	8.2	0	0	7.5	8.4	5.9

Science Companions 1 © A Porter, M Wood, T Wood and Stanley Thornes (Publishers) Ltd, 1991

c) Which city had more rain that week?
d) What was the total number of hours of sunshine for the week in Belfast?
e) What was the total number of hours of sunshine for the week in London?
f) Which city was the sunnier that week?
g) Draw three bar charts, one for rainfall, one for maximum temperature and one for sunshine. Put the figures for both Belfast and London on the same charts. Use graph paper if possible, or sketch rough charts.

5. Look at the activities in the 'Try it yourself' section which follows.
a) When setting up a rain gauge, why should you have the top at least 30 cm off the ground?
b) Why should the rain gauge be set up in the open and not under trees?
c) Why should the top of the rain gauge be the same width as the part with the scale on?
d) When measuring the temperature, why is the thermometer set up in a shady spot rather than in direct sunlight?

Research

1. There is a great deal of folklore concerning the weather. Read up about this and see if you can use the ideas to predict the weather.

Try it yourself

1. Keep a weather diary. Note the cloud types you see, the rainfall every 24 hours, the wind directions, and the shade temperatures. Below are some practical ideas:

Making a rain gauge
Use an old coffee jar or similar container whose neck is the same width as the main part of the jar. Fix a scale in millimetres on to the side of it. Glue the bottle on to a wooden block. Place it in the middle of a wide open space so that the top is at least 30 cm above the ground. Fix the block in the ground to hold the jar steady. Measure the rainfall every 24 hours for as many weeks as possible.

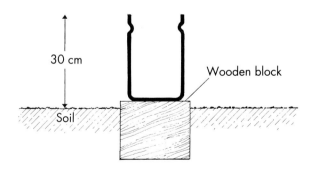

30 cm

Wooden block

Soil

Taking the temperature
Set up a thermometer in the shade and record the temperature at least daily, or better still in the morning, at noon, in the afternoon and just before going to bed.

Measuring the wind direction
You can simply use a compass, and hold a handkerchief up in the wind. This will give you an approximate wind direction. (In fact, true north is about 8 degrees to the east of magnetic north.) Alternatively you can construct a simple wind vane as shown below.

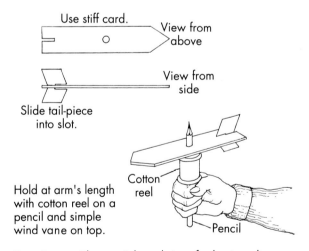

Use stiff card.
View from above
View from side
Slide tail-piece into slot.

Hold at arm's length with cotton reel on a pencil and simple wind vane on top.
Cotton reel
Pencil

Experiment with materials and sizes for best results.

2. Devise a simple apparatus to measure wind speed.

3. Air pressure may be measured using an **aneroid barometer**. This contains a small corrugated metal cylinder with low air pressure inside. Changes in the outside air pressure cause the lid to move. Try to build a simple barometer using a jam jar, balloon, straw and scale.

21

Climate and farming

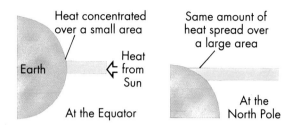

Heat concentrated over a small area

Earth

Heat from Sun

At the Equator

Same amount of heat spread over a large area

At the North Pole

North ← HIGH → Hadley cell ← LOW → Hadley cell ← HIGH → South

↑←2000 miles→↑ ↑←2000 miles→↑
Tropic of Cancer   Equator   Tropic of Capricorn

Weather is the changes which happen in the air around you every day. **Climate** describes the weather pattern at a place over a period of 30 years.

The climate is influenced by several factors including the energy from the Sun, the Earth's shape and position in space, the spin of the Earth, the atmosphere and the oceans.

At the Equator the heat from the Sun is more concentrated than at the poles, because of the curve of the Earth's surface.

At the Equator the hot air rises, causing huge convection currents. These convection currents produce areas in the atmosphere known as the **Hadley cells**. They are named after George Hadley (1685–1768). He was a British weather expert who suggested that it was the rotation of the Earth as well as the Sun's heat which caused the major air movements.

The rising hot air produces low pressure at the Earth's surface, and lots of rain. The air cools and descends about 2000 miles north or south of the Equator. This descending air causes high pressure. The air is dry because it lost its water when it rose at the Equator, so there are deserts in these high-pressure areas.

These deserts include the Sahara in Africa and the deserts of Western Australia and south-west Africa (Namibia). They are inhabited by two types of people. Some are **nomadic** (wandering from place to place) whilst others live in **oases** – areas where water is available. Careful irrigation using water from wells enables crops to be grown such as wheat, maize, rice and date palms.

The tropical rainforest of the Amazon, South-east Asia and Zaire all receive over 240 cm of rain a year with average temperatures over 24 °C. This makes them highly productive areas. However, people are cutting down hardwood trees such as mahogany, teak and balsa. They grow crops such as cocoa which need the heat and moisture of the tropical climate. The cleared land only yields crops for three or four years due to lack of humus or fertiliser. Nutrients in the soil are leached (washed away) by heavy rain.

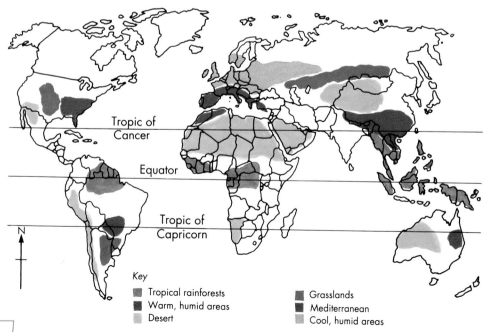

Tropic of Cancer

Equator

Tropic of Capricorn

N

Key
- ■ Tropical rainforests
- ■ Warm, humid areas
- ■ Desert
- ■ Grasslands
- ■ Mediterranean
- ■ Cool, humid areas

The warm, humid climates of the south-eastern United States and large areas of China produce many crops per year. Here there is warmth and regular rainfall.

The climate of the Mediterranean is warm and dry in the summer with mild wet winters. It is a highly productive area if there is good irrigation.

Most of Europe is cool and humid. So far north, the Sun's energy is starting to spread out and weaken. The humidity is caused by the **North Atlantic Drift**, an ocean current which comes from the Caribbean. The prevailing wind is also from that area so rainfall can be high, particularly west of mountains. Clouds rise over the mountains. This cools the air which means it cannot hold as much water vapour. Water vapour condenses and falls as rain. The land to the east of the hills is in a 'rain shadow' as the clouds have lost most of their water on the western side.

Seasonal changes are caused by the tilt of the Earth on its axis. In our summer, areas north of the Equator are closer to the Sun so are warmer (see *Try it yourself 1* on pages 16–17). This means that Atlantic depressions move on a path to the north of the UK giving us warmer, more stable air. In our winter, areas south of the Equator are nearer the Sun so are warmer. The depressions' paths move south and are then over the UK, giving us cooler, wetter, more changeable weather. Europe's crops are influenced by the cold winters, low levels of sunlight and the short dry summers.

The grain areas of the world are also the great cattle lands. Rainfall is low and uncertain in summer. These grasslands are the plains and prairies of North America, the pampas of South America and the steppes of Russia.

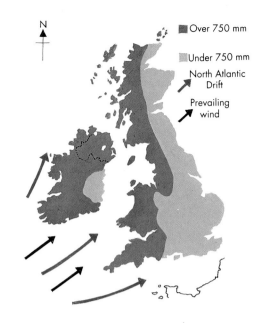

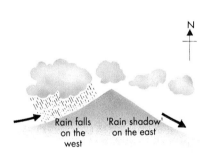

Rain falls on the west | 'Rain shadow' on the east

Catastrophic events

Tides and tidal surges
Tides are caused by the gravitational pull of the Moon and, to a lesser extent, the Sun. When these both pull in the same direction very high tides called **spring tides** occur. A good example is the Severn Bore, which may be used in the future as an energy source. Occasionally, if strong winds and high tides occur together the combined results can be catastrophic, as happened on 31 January 1953. The sea surged over 2 metres in the narrow Thames estuary and caused major flooding at Canvey Island. The Thames Barrier was built to stop such flooding.

Rain
Heavy rain can cause floods. The city of York has been flooded on numerous occasions. Recently, Yorkshire Water built defences which they believe will help prevent flooding.

QUESTIONS

1. Why is the Earth hotter at the Equator than near the poles?
2. Why is there heavy rain around the Equator?
3. Name three areas of tropical rainforest.
4. What is a 'rain shadow'?
5. What causes tides?

1. Sir Francis Beaufort (1774–1857) was born in Ireland. He joined the Royal Navy as a young man and served for over 20 years. In 1806 he put forward the idea of the Beaufort scale to measure wind speed. In those days the idea was to state the amount of sail a ship should carry at each wind speed. Thirty years later it was officially adopted by the Admiralty. In 1829 he became hydrographer to the Royal Navy (a hydrographer is someone who studies water on the Earth's surface such as in the oceans, rivers and lakes).

Beaufort scale number	Wind	Effects	Speed in knots (1 knot is 1.15 land m.p.h.)
0	Calm	Smoke rises vertically	0
1	Light air	Smoke drifts in wind	1 – 3
2	Light breeze	Wind felt on face, leaves rustle, weather vanes move	4 – 6
3	Gentle breeze	Light flag blows, leaves and small twigs move	7 – 10
4	Moderate breeze	Small branches move, dust and loose paper blow	11 – 16
5	Fresh breeze	Small trees sway, waves seen on ponds, etc.	17 – 21
6	Strong breeze	Large branches move, telephone wires whistle	22 – 27
7	Moderate gale	Hard to walk into the wind, trees start to sway	28 – 33
8	Fresh gale	Very hard to walk into wind, twigs break off trees	34 – 40
9	Strong gale	Structural damage probable, slates and chimney pots lost	41 – 47
10	Whole gale	Trees uprooted, serious damage to buildings	48 – 55
11	Storm	Very rare inland, causes widespread damage	56 – 63
12	Hurricane	Major disaster	64 – 71

a) Where and in what year was Francis Beaufort born?
b) When was the Beaufort scale invented?
c) When was the scale adopted by the Navy?

For the following questions, study the cartoons and suggest which number on the Beaufort scale could best be used to indicate the wind speed.

d)   e)   f)

Gilbert wrecks the Caribbean

WORLD NEWS

2. Read the newspaper article carefully, and then answer the questions which follow.

500 000 people were made homeless in Jamaica when Hurricane Gilbert passed over the island on 12 September 1988. One day later it reached the Cayman Islands, where winds of 208 km/h were reported, and it was given a Category 4 status. After another 24 hours it became a Category 5, the strongest category of hurricane, with winds of 280 km/h. At its strongest Gilbert used more power in a day than the United States uses in a whole year. The eye of the storm had narrowed to 18 km of clear air. Here was recorded the lowest ever air pressure for the Atlantic, 884 mb.

This hospital was devastated by Hurricane Gilbert

Date	Local time	Sustained wind speed (km/h)
10	1600	64
11	0400	112
11	1600	128
12	0400	160
12	1600	176
13	0400	184
13	1600	208
14	0400	256
14	1600	280
15	0400	224
15	1600	125
16	0400	192
16	1600	192
17	0400	192
17	1600	104

a) How many people were made homeless in Jamaica?
b) What was the lowest recorded Atlantic air pressure?
c) What was the diameter of the eye of the storm at its smallest size?

d) How much power was used by Gilbert in a day?
e) Use the table on the left to plot a bar chart of the sustained wind speed in km/h against time every 12 hours.

3. Climate, type of landscape, soil and temperature all influence farming. Study the two maps of the UK below and then answer the questions.

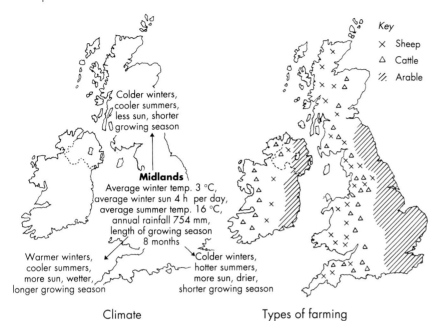

Colder winters, cooler summers, less sun, shorter growing season

Midlands
Average winter temp. 3 °C, average winter sun 4 h per day, average summer temp. 16 °C, annual rainfall 754 mm, length of growing season 8 months

Warmer winters, cooler summers, more sun, wetter, longer growing season

Colder winters, hotter summers, more sun, drier, shorter growing season

Climate

Key
× Sheep
△ Cattle
// Arable

Types of farming

a) Suggest why sheep and cattle are reared in the western regions of the UK, whilst arable farming, in general, happens on the eastern side.
b) Why does south-west England have a warmer winter and cooler summer than south-east England?
c) Why does the west of Ireland get heavy rainfall?
d) Why is it possible to grow many types of palm tree and other 'tropical' plants on the west coast of Scotland?

4. Read the following newspaper article carefully, and then answer the questions which follow.

WORLD NEWS
Towyn mops up
The big clean-up started in Towyn, North Wales, yesterday as soon as the breach in the sea wall had been repaired. 30 000 tonnes of Armorstone boulders were used along with an equal quantity of concrete.

Unfortunately, 20% of the residents of Towyn and Kinmela were not covered by insurance for their house contents.

It may take four months for all the residents to return home because of structural damage to property. A police spokesperson said that many residents were insisting on returning despite the condition of their property. 'The sea has a lot to answer for' was one comment heard yesterday.

(5.3.90)

a) Where is Towyn?
b) What materials were used to repair the sea wall?
c) Which town, apart from Towyn, is mentioned in the article?
d) What percentage of residents were not covered by home contents insurance?
e) How long may it be before the residents can return to safe homes?
f) What was the initial cause of the damage to the sea wall?

5. Study the following information about catastrophic winds and then answer the questions which follow.

Tornado in Kansas, USA

Cyclones start in the western Atlantic Ocean. They are like super-low pressure regions with winds circulating at 200 km/h. The energy from the Sun is great here. This means water evaporates very quickly. This causes thunderstorms, as energy is transferred from the water to the air. Cyclones may develop into **hurricanes**.
Hurricanes may be hundreds of kilometres across, but **tornadoes** are only a few hundred metres wide. Winds twist around the centre at up to 500 km/h. This makes such a low pressure at the centre that buildings in their paths explode as the tornado, or 'twister', passes over them.

a) Where do cyclones start?
b) How fast can winds move in a cyclone?
c) Why does water evaporate quickly in a cyclone?
d) How do hurricanes and tornadoes differ in size?
e) How much faster are wind speeds in a tornado than in a cyclone?
f) Why is a 'twister' a good name for a tornado?

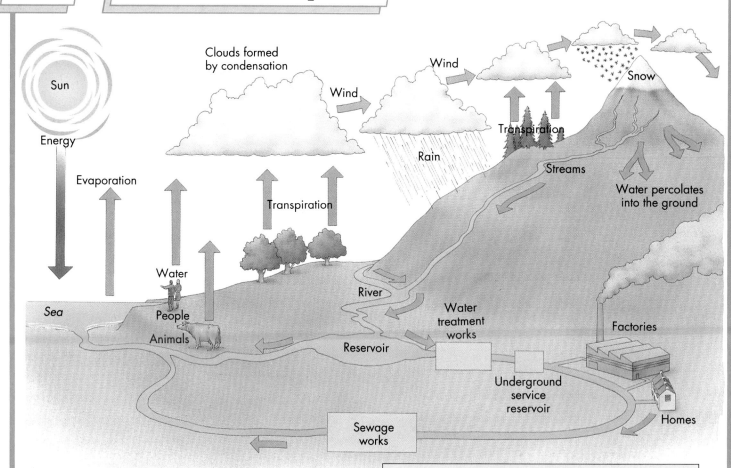

Two-thirds of the surface of the Earth is covered by water. This water moves around in different forms. The water cycle above shows how this happens.

Energy from the Sun makes some of the water in the sea evaporate. The water vapour rises into the air where it condenses into clouds. The clouds rise over high ground and cool down, because air is colder higher up. The clouds get so cold that they can no longer keep their water as vapour and so it falls to Earth as rain or snow.

Moisture also gets into the air from animals and plants. When animals breathe out they give out a lot of water. Trees and plants also lose water into the air by a process called **transpiration**.

Some water runs over the ground into streams and rivers and then back to the sea if people do not use it. Some water soaks into the ground where it percolates slowly down to the sea or into wells and boreholes. The level at which water settles underground is known as the **water table**.

Facts about the water cycle

- 97% of all the Earth's water is salty. Under 3% is fresh, and most of this is trapped in the polar ice caps. The air, rivers, lakes and underground areas store less than 1%.
- Each year about 40 000 cubic kilometres of water blow over the land as clouds of water vapour and are returned to the sea.
- People need water to live and produce goods. Before we use water it has to pass through a water treatment works to make it safe.

Facts about the use of water

Homes (domestic use)
Each person uses per day:

Car and garden	5 litres
Laundry	16 litres
Washing and bathing	23 litres
Flushing the toilet	36 litres
Drinking, cooking and washing up	40 litres

Industry

1 tonne of bread needs	4000 litres
1 tonne of sugar needs	8000 litres
1 tonne of steel needs	112 000 litres
1 tonne of nylon needs	140 000 litres
1 tonne of paper needs	225 000 litres

A water treatment works

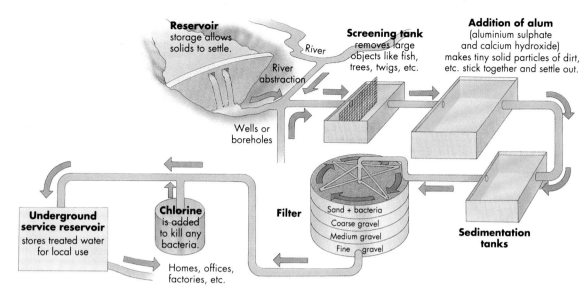

Reservoir storage allows solids to settle.

River

River abstraction

Wells or boreholes

Screening tank removes large objects like fish, trees, twigs, etc.

Addition of alum (aluminium sulphate and calcium hydroxide) makes tiny solid particles of dirt, etc. stick together and settle out.

Underground service reservoir stores treated water for local use

Chlorine is added to kill any bacteria.

Filter

Sand + bacteria
Coarse gravel
Medium gravel
Fine gravel

Sedimentation tanks

Homes, offices, factories, etc.

A sewage treatment plant

After homes, factories, schools and offices have used the water it must be purified before being returned to the sea. This purification happens at a sewage treatment plant.

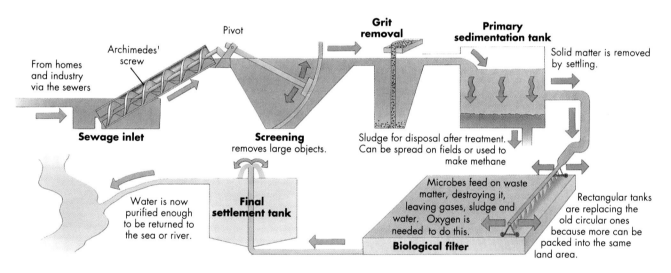

Pivot

Grit removal

Primary sedimentation tank

Solid matter is removed by settling.

From homes and industry via the sewers

Archimedes' screw

Sewage inlet

Screening removes large objects.

Sludge for disposal after treatment. Can be spread on fields or used to make methane

Microbes feed on waste matter, destroying it, leaving gases, sludge and water. Oxygen is needed to do this.

Biological filter

Rectangular tanks are replacing the old circular ones because more can be packed into the same land area.

Water is now purified enough to be returned to the sea or river.

Final settlement tank

The sewerage system

This is the underground network of pipes needed to transport domestic and industrial sewage to the treatment works.

Sewerage systems began to be built in the nineteenth century because of the high death rate from water-borne diseases such as typhoid, cholera and types of dysentery. The average life of a sewer is about 100 years, so constant maintenance or replacement is required.

Sewers may vary in size from 15 cm to over 250 cm in diameter.

QUESTIONS

1. Name the process by which water vapour gets into the atmosphere.

2. What is the meaning of the phrase 'water percolates slowly down to the sea'?

3. Name the main ways people remove water from the natural water cycle.

4. Why is chlorine gas added to drinking water?

1. Here are six pairs of words. They are written so that the last letter of the first word becomes the first letter of the second word. Two clues are provided for each pair. The shaded square represents the letter which is in both words. For example,

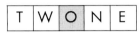

T W O N E

The words are two and one.

On your own copy, complete the squares using the clues below.

a) Two water-borne diseases mentioned in 'The sewerage system'. The words are linked by the fourth letter of the alphabet.

b) This is what water does when it trickles down through the ground. The process for removing large objects from water or sewage.

c) A third water-borne disease. The process of removing water from a river for treatment.

d) A type of well to obtain water. The process by which water leaves the sea and goes into the air, helped by the Sun and wind.

e) A large body of water stored ready for use. A large body of running water.

f) A famous scientist who invented a 'screw' for raising water. The system of underground pipes to carry waste.

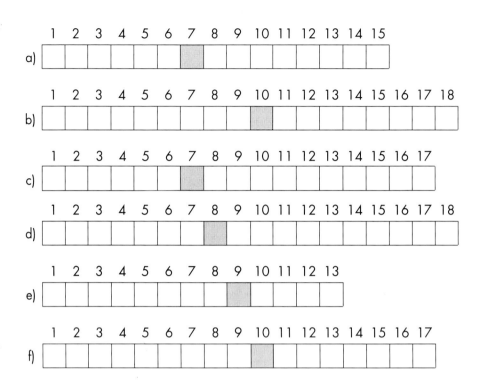

a) 1 2 3 4 5 6 7 8 9 10 11 12 13 14 15

b) 1 2 3 4 5 6 7 8 9 10 11 12 13 14 15 16 17 18

c) 1 2 3 4 5 6 7 8 9 10 11 12 13 14 15 16 17

d) 1 2 3 4 5 6 7 8 9 10 11 12 13 14 15 16 17 18

e) 1 2 3 4 5 6 7 8 9 10 11 12 13

f) 1 2 3 4 5 6 7 8 9 10 11 12 13 14 15 16 17

2. Read the following newspaper article, then answer the questions which follow.

WORLD NEWS (16.2.90)
Perrier problems

Benzene is a liquid which is known to cause cancer. It has been found in bottles of Perrier water. The company has acted quickly – all production has been stopped, and all bottles of Perrier worldwide have been withdrawn from sale. This has cost the company millions of pounds.

The carbon dioxide which gives Perrier its fizz comes from deep in the ground. It forces its way to the surface through cracks in the rocks. It dissolves in the water as it rises towards the surface. On the way it passes through rocks which contain dead plants. This is where the benzene is picked up.

Near the surface, the company separates the water and carbon dioxide. The carbon dioxide is passed through charcoal filters to remove the benzene and other impurities. It is believed that the benzene has appeared because the company failed to maintain the filters. The pure carbon dioxide is then reinjected into the water. There is 3.5 times as much gas as water in Perrier.

In Britain alone, 1989 saw the sale of 250 million litres of mineral water. Of these sales, Perrier have over 50% of the market.

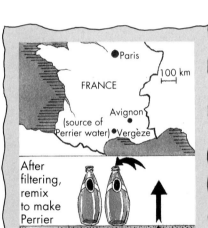

●Paris

FRANCE

|—100 km

Avignon

(source of Perrier water) ●Vergèze

After filtering, remix to make Perrier

Clay

Sand containing the water

Carbon dioxide from below dissolves in the water

Rocks which contain plants that lived millions of years ago

Limestone and other carbonate rocks

Carbon dioxide rises through cracks in rocks

Magma from deep in the Earth

Science Companions 1 © A Porter, M Wood, T Wood and Stanley Thornes (Publishers) Ltd, 1991

a) Where, deep in the Earth, is the carbon dioxide produced?

b) What is the first type of rock through which the carbon dioxide passes?

c) Where is it thought the carbon dioxide picks up the benzene?

d) Why is benzene dangerous?

e) What is used to remove benzene and other impurities?

f) How many litres of gas are there in a one-litre bottle of Perrier?

g) How many litres of mineral water were sold in Britain in 1989?

h) What is the difference between mineral water and tap water?

3. Read the newspaper article below, then answer the questions which follow.

WORLD NEWS (16.3.90)

New York splashes water in Perrier's face

New York is not usually thought of as a clean city. However, recent problems with Perrier water have made New Yorkers smile. In restaurants in the city, Perrier can cost £12 per gallon. Tap water works out at 60p for 750 gallons, and it is safe to drink! The water is brought to the city from the Catskill Mountains some 170 km away. Huge underground pipes and tunnels are used to deliver the 1.2 billion gallons a day which New York uses. The system works by gravity, so it never fails.

It is 70 years since the New York water system was switched on. Plans are now well advanced to switch it off in order to check the 4.5 m wide tunnels which are over 200 m beneath the city. Today a new 7.3 m diameter tunnel, lined with concrete, is being built. By the end of the twentieth century it will be ready, and then the present tunnels will be closed, one at a time, for maintenance. Each tunnel is expected to take 10 years to check.

The new tunnel has taken 20 years to build, cost £1.8 billion and is 19 km long. It is up to 240 m underground. It should be free from trouble and last for 200 years.

The water can be turned off by large taps called valves. The valves on the old system are made of brass. The new system has valves made of stainless steel. Each valve is 2.4 m across and there are 17 pairs of them. They are normally worked by electricity, but in an emergency can be operated by hand, in which case they would take 9 hours to close.

a) What is the cost of Perrier water, per litre, in New York? (One gallon contains 4.5 litres.)

b) Where does New York City's water come from, and over what distance?

c) How old is the present New York water distribution system?

d) How much bigger in diameter is the new tunnel than the old ones?

e) Why has the water distribution system never failed?

f) For how long is the new tunnel expected to last?

g) How many gallons of water are used in New York in a week?

h) Suggest why the new tunnel is being lined with concrete.

4. On your own copy, complete the eight horizontal words using the following clues (a) to (h). Then answer part (i).

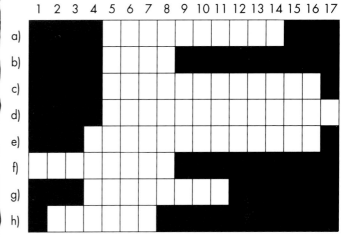

a) A filter which relies on living organisms to destroy waste matter.

b) This is added to remove tiny particles of solid by making them stick together.

c) Clouds are formed by this process.

d) Trees lose water to the air by this process.

e) A tank where large particles of solid settle out.

f) A yellow–green gas added to water to kill bacteria.

g) The living organisms used in the filter in (a) above.

h) The waste product which travels in the sewerage system.

i) Now find the word in column 5.

Science Companions 1 © A Porter, M Wood, T Wood and Stanley Thornes (Publishers) Ltd, 1991

The structure of the Earth

The Earth is made of a central **core** which runs from the centre to about 2900 km below the surface. In the core, which is liquid, temperatures may reach 4500 °C.

The **mantle** floats on top of the core, beneath the crust. Temperatures here may reach 3800 °C. About 250 km below the crust the mantle begins to turn molten. This means that the crust is floating on a very thick liquid.

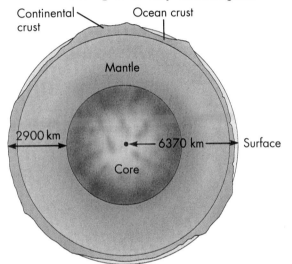

Continental crust — Ocean crust
Mantle
2900 km — 6370 km — Surface
Core

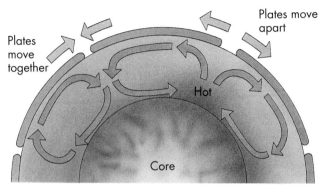

Plates move apart
Plates move together
Hot
Core

The crust is the surface of the Earth. It is thicker where there is land. This **continental crust** is made of granite rock and is between 20 and 65 km thick. The **ocean crust** is only 5 to 10 km thick. It forms the ocean floor and is made of heavy basalt rock.

The temperature varies in the mantle – there are hotter and cooler areas. This causes convection currents which move the mantle around, very slowly. These currents move the crust. The crust is split into large areas called **plates**. The movements of these plates cause earthquakes and volcanoes.

Plate movements and earthquakes

When two plates move against each other, the Earth's surface changes. One effect is to **fold** the Earth's surface.

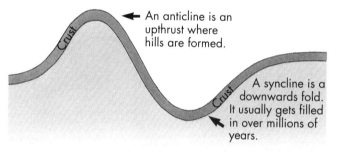

Crust ← An anticline is an upthrust where hills are formed.

A syncline is a downwards fold. It usually gets filled in over millions of years. Crust

Another effect of plates moving together is an **earthquake**. Earthquakes are centred at one point called the **epicentre**. The energy moves outwards in all directions in waves called **seismic waves**, like the waves when a stone is dropped into a pond. The size or magnitude of an earthquake is measured on the **Richter scale**.

The San Andreas Fault is probably the most famous point in the world where plates meet. San Francisco lies on this fault. The city was destroyed by a major earthquake in 1906. The destruction was caused mainly by fires from broken gas mains. In 1989 another earthquake struck. The new 'quake-proof' skyscrapers rocked as designed, but a double-decker highway collapsed.

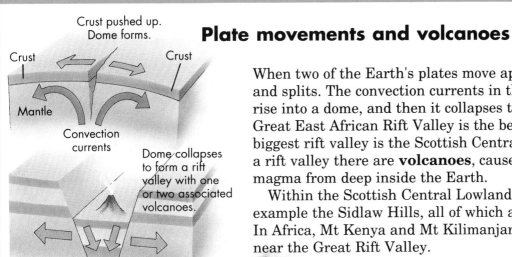

Crust pushed up.
Dome forms.

Crust   Crust

Mantle

Convection
currents

Dome collapses
to form a rift
valley with one
or two associated
volcanoes.

Formation of a rift valley

Plate movements and volcanoes

EARTH AND ATMOSPHERE

When two of the Earth's plates move apart, the crust stretches and splits. The convection currents in the mantle make the crust rise into a dome, and then it collapses to form a **rift valley**. The Great East African Rift Valley is the best example. Britain's biggest rift valley is the Scottish Central Lowland. Within or near a rift valley there are **volcanoes**, caused by the upward thrust of magma from deep inside the Earth.

Within the Scottish Central Lowland are five ranges of hills, for example the Sidlaw Hills, all of which are peaks of volcanic rock. In Africa, Mt Kenya and Mt Kilimanjaro are both old volcanoes near the Great Rift Valley.

The acid lava volcano

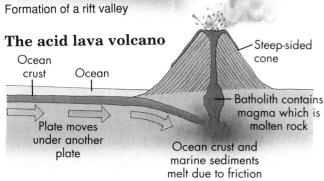

This type of volcano is formed where one of the Earth's plates slides under another. An example is Mt Etna, Sicily. The crust melts as it descends into the mantle. It forms a thick **acid magma** which rises slowly. This slow-moving magma forms steep-sided cones because it solidifies quickly as it leaves the crater. Magma is called **lava** when it is on the surface of the Earth.

The basic lava volcano

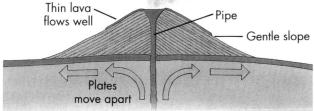

This type forms where two plates are moving apart, or as in Mauna Loa, Hawaii, where magma rises to a 'hot spot' under the ocean crust. The magma comes from molten rock which is thin. It is called **basic magma**. This thin lava flows well and allows gentle eruptions. After coming out of the pipe it forms gentle sloping cones known as **shield cones**.

Ash and lava deposits from a volcano eventually produce a nutrient-rich soil which is ideal for farming.

The destruction of Pompeii

In AD 79, Mt Vesuvius erupted and destroyed the cities of Pompeii and Herculaneum. About 20 000 people died. Pompeii was buried beneath ash and Herculaneum was destroyed by a flow of boiling mud. At Pompeii the ash preserved the bodies of the citizens, many of which have been uncovered over the past 250 years since the city was rediscovered in 1748.

QUESTIONS

1. From what type of rock is the ocean crust made?
2. Name the fault upon which San Francisco is built.
3. Name two rift valleys.
4. What scale is used to measure the strength of earthquakes?
5. Why is the eruption more gentle from a basic lava volcano than from an acid lava volcano?
6. What is the large dome of magma called under an acid lava volcano?

31

1. Read the following passage carefully, then answer the questions which follow.

The strength of an earthquake is called its **magnitude**. It is measured on the **Richter scale**. Charles Francis Richter (1900–85) was born in Butler County, Ohio, USA. In 1935 he devised the scale which bears his name.

As earthquakes move up the scale a number at a time, they get 10 times stronger. This means that an earthquake of magnitude 4 is ten times as strong as one of magnitude 3. The strongest recorded earthquake was that in Lisbon in 1755 which is said to have measured 8.9 on the Richter scale.

Magnitude on the Richter scale	Effect of earthquake	Average number per year worldwide
2–3	Only shows on seismometers	300 000
3–4	Slight – like heavy traffic	50 000
4–5	Moderate – sleepers awake, church bells ring	6000
5–6	Strong – walls crack, plaster falls	800
6–7	Ground cracks, some buildings fall	130
7–8	Disastrous – most buildings collapse, landslides	20
8–9	Catastrophic – total destruction, ground rises and falls in waves	1

Some major twentieth-century earthquakes

Date	Place	Magnitude	Deaths
1906	San Francisco, USA	8.3	700
1964	Alaska, USA	8.5	178
1968	Iran	7.4	12 000
1976	China	7.8	242 000
1983	Japan	7.7	58
1985	Mexico	8.1	4290
1988	America, USSR	7.0	25 000

Earthquakes are recorded on a **seismograph**. As the Earth moves, the pen moves over a piece of paper and produces a trace showing how violent the earthquake has been.

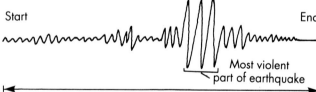

Start   End

Most violent part of earthquake

5 seconds

Earthquakes are rare in Britain, or certainly strong ones which we can feel. On Monday 2 April 1990 a tremor centred at Wrexham in North Wales occurred with a magnitude of 5.2. Its effects were felt as far away as Liverpool and Pwllheli. In Liverpool some chimney pots fell down.

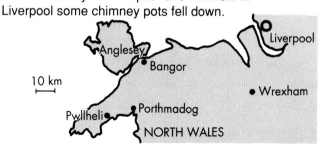

Liverpool
Anglesey
Bangor
10 km
Wrexham
Pwllheli
Porthmadog
NORTH WALES

a) Who invented the scale which measures the strength of earthquakes?

b) When was it invented?

c) How many times stronger is an earthquake of magnitude 8 than one of magnitude 6?

d) Where and when was the strongest recorded earthquake, and what was its strength?

e) Why is it not possible to be certain of the exact strength of the earthquake mentioned in (d)?

f) What instrument is used to record an earthquake?

g) Seven earthquakes are given in the table of twentieth-century earthquakes.

 i) List them by place name in order from weakest to strongest.

 ii) List them by place name in order from smallest to largest number of deaths.

h) Where did the British earthquake occur in 1990?

i) What effect did this earthquake have in Liverpool?

J) What was its strength on the Richter scale?

k) Using the data given, write a paragraph to describe an eyewitness account of the 1988 Armenian earthquake.

l) Draw a Richter scale which shows the damage in pictures rather than words.

Science Companions 1 © A Porter, M Wood, T Wood and Stanley Thornes (Publishers) Ltd, 1991

2. Study the world map shown below. List the 12 names of the volcanoes shown on the map. Use an atlas or other reference book to find out in which country each volcano is found.

3. Study the newspaper article below, then answer the questions which follow.

WORLD NEWS (20.5.80)
Volcanic hazards predictions
The major eruption of Mt St Helens two days ago was preceded by several clues which may help to predict future eruptions at other sites. March saw an increase in the number of small earthquakes. April produced some minor eruptions and the formation of some new craters. Early May saw a large bulge, some 100 metres high, appear on the north face; snow and ice melted and local animals started behaving very strangely. A strong earthquake happened just before the major eruption.

a) What was the date of the major eruption of Mt St Helens?
b) What was the probable cause of the 100-metre-high bulge?
c) Why did the ice and snow begin to melt?
d) Why did local animals start behaving strangely?
e) Suggest why some local people died, despite the area being sealed off.

4. The squares below represent the name of a Mexican volcano. It erupted in April 1982, sending millions of tonnes of ash into the air.

a)	b)		c)	d)	e)	f)	g)	h)	i)

Use the clues below to find the name of the volcano. Write the one-word answer for each clue. Then, on your own copy, fill in the first letter of each answer in the grid, and you will have the name of the volcano.
a) The name given to the shaking of the Earth. (10)
b) A large flow of 'liquid' from a volcano. (4)
c) The top layer of the Earth, upon which we stand. (5)
d) These are formed on an anticline. (5)
e) This melted before Mt St Helens erupted. (3)
f) The San Andreas Fault passes through this US state. (10)
g) In the mantle, the opposite of cold. (3)
h) A large sea. (5)
i) Ash and lava produce a soil rich in these. (9)

33

Weathering and landscaping

Weathering of buildings

Most modern buildings are made of brick and concrete, though a few are still built from natural stone. Sandstone has attractive soft red or gold colours and is easy to carve. Limestone is the most popular natural building stone in Britain. Unfortunately, both sandstone and limestone are easily weathered by **acid rain**. The burning of fossil fuels releases gases into the air which make the rain acidic (see section 4.2). The results can often be seen on churches – statues which have survived hundreds of years have been eaten away rapidly in the polluted air of the last 100 years.

Gargoyle at Lincoln Cathedral before acid rain...   ... and after

Landscaping

Water/ice

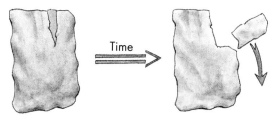

Time

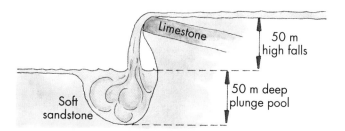

Limestone

50 m high falls

Soft sandstone

50 m deep plunge pool

Water expands when it freezes. When water gets into cracks in rocks and freezes, it opens the cracks. Over several winters this causes pieces of rock to fall away. These form a pile of **scree** at the bottom of a rock face.

Rainfall can wash away surface soil – it **erodes** the soil. The roots of plants and trees help to stop this by binding the soil together. Where forests and other surface vegetation are cleared, soil can be washed off slopes and deposited on flat land below.

Erosion on deforested land, Amazon

Rivers shape the land in many ways. Layers of hard rock resist erosion by rivers, while soft rock is eaten away. Niagara Falls are so powerful that the cliffs are being eroded backwards and up-river by 1 metre every year. Over millions of years the river has carved a gorge 11 kilometres long.

The mighty Colorado river has cut out the Grand Canyon in Arizona, USA, over millions of years. It is over 1 kilometre deep. The sides are steep because of the resistance of harder rocks.

On flat land, rivers meander in a series of bends, flowing too gently to dig deep canyons. Here they change the landscape by wearing away land on the outsides of the bends. This material is then deposited further downstream on the insides of bends.

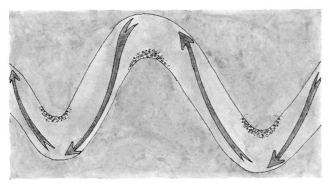

The River Nile has created a huge delta at its mouth in Egypt. It carries mud as it flows and drops this as it enters the Mediterranean Sea. There is little or no tide in the Mediterranean Sea so the mud stays where it is deposited. The delta has built up over millions of years.

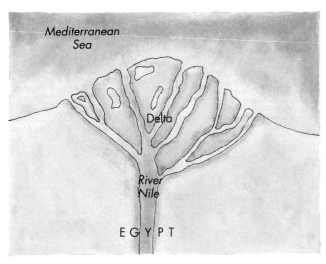

The sea is a powerful force which can erode the coast very quickly. In storms it can destroy sea defences in minutes. Even in calmer times it still affects the land. Over millions of years it wears away cliffs and creates caves, arches and other unusual shapes.

The Green Bridge of Wales, Pembrokeshire

The wind plays a part in shaping rocks too. There are many natural arches made of sandstone which have been eroded by the wind in the western United States. It has been calculated that a windstorm can carry up to a million tonnes of material for more than 3000 kilometres. When this material hits soft rocks it can weather them into strange shapes.

QUESTIONS

1. Name two important natural building materials in Britain.
2. What is a scree, and how has it been produced?
3. How do trees and grasses prevent soil erosion?
4. How fast are the cliffs being eroded at Niagara Falls?
5. Why has the Nile Delta grown?
6. How does wind cause erosion?

1. Study the following information and then answer the questions which follow.

How soils are made

Weathering breaks rocks down into very small pieces which become part of the soil.

Grain sizes differ in different soils. A **sandy soil** drains well because it has large grains with big spaces between them. A **clay soil** drains badly because the grains have a flat shape with small spaces between them.

A **soil profile** shows the layers of different materials down to the parent rock. The layers are called **horizons**.

A fertile soil is good for farming and gardening. It should contain a lot of rotted vegetation called **humus**, and be a **loam soil**. Loam soils contain different sizes of grains.

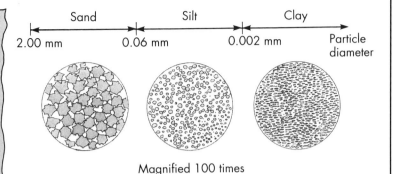

Magnified 100 times

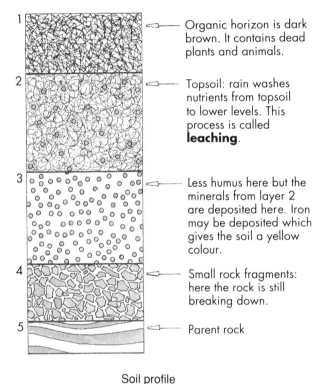

1 — Organic horizon is dark brown. It contains dead plants and animals.

2 — Topsoil: rain washes nutrients from topsoil to lower levels. This process is called **leaching**.

3 — Less humus here but the minerals from layer 2 are deposited here. Iron may be deposited which gives the soil a yellow colour.

4 — Small rock fragments: here the rock is still breaking down.

5 — Parent rock

Soil profile

a) Which type of soil has the largest grain sizes?
b) Why does this type of soil drain best?
c) What name is given to the different layers in a soil profile?
d) What is humus?
e) Why do you think the best soil contains particles of various sizes?
f) What is leaching?

2. Crushed samples of dry soils were placed in filter funnels in the tops of measuring cylinders as shown below. Equal volumes of soil and water were used in each experiment. Study the diagrams and then answer the questions which follow.

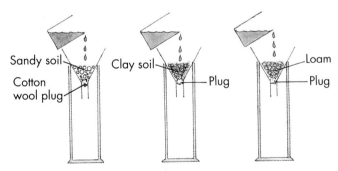

a) On your own copy, fill in the results table opposite using these possible results:

Times: 10 s, 50 s, 500 s

Volumes after 30 minutes: 0.5 cm³, 30 cm³, 45 cm³

b) Why were the soil samples dry to start with?
c) Why were the soil samples crushed?

Results	Sandy soil	Clay soil	Loam
Time taken for the first drop of water to fall into the cylinder (seconds)			
Volume of water in the cylinder after 30 minutes (cm³)			

Science Companions 1 © A Porter, M Wood, T Wood and Stanley Thornes (Publishers) Ltd, 1991

3. Study the following information about the River Nile, and then answer the questions.

The River Nile in Egypt used to carry a lot of mud, called silt, with it. In 1970 the Aswan High Dam was completed and the quantity of mud in the river fell.

Before entering Egypt, the Nile flows through the Ethiopian Highlands. At Egypt's southern boundary it is held behind the Aswan High Dam, and forms Lake Nasser which is almost 500 km long.

Below are the silt readings (in parts per million) taken 100 km downstream of the Aswan High Dam site in 1889 and 1989.

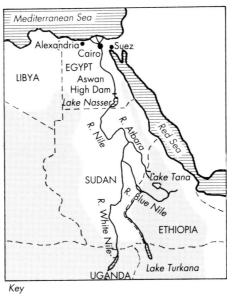

Key

Ground over 500 m

a) On separate sheets of graph paper, draw bar charts to show the silt readings in 1889 and 1989.
b) What do you think may happen in the Ethiopian Highlands between June and October, as shown by the 1889 figures?
c) Why did the silt not travel down the river in 1989?
d) Where do you think the silt went in 1989?
e) Why do you think the Nile Delta has started to erode.

	Jan	Feb	Mar	Apr	May	Jun	Jul	Aug	Sept	Oct	Nov	Dec
1889	60	50	40	45	45	90	700	2700	2400	900	130	75
1989	45	46	45	50	50	48	47	45	44	46	47	46

Try it yourself

1. Take a note pad, and a camera if you have one, into your local town and look for examples of weathering on buildings. Where you find an example make records, such as:
a) Note the exact location.
b) Make a sketch or photograph with notes to support it.
c) See if you can find out which stone or building materials were used.
d) How old is the building? (There may be a dated information stone or plaque.)

2. Try testing the pH of soil. Shake some soil with a little pure water. Allow the water to stand and let the soil settle. Then test with Universal Indicator paper to find the pH.

3. Find an old clear glass jar, the bigger the better, with a tight-fitting lid. Dig up a narrow strip of soil about 30 cm deep. Place it in the jar so that the jar is about one-third full. Add water to fill the jar. Put the top on and shake thoroughly. Allow to settle for at least a day. Draw and write about what you can see.

4. *Soil characteristics*
Study the list below. Take a handful of soil from near your home and examine it carefully. See whether it fits one of these soil types, or more likely, is between types. Does all your class get the same results?

Sandy
Coarse and gritty to the touch
Sand particles can be seen
Cannot be made to stick into a ball
Hand left fairly clean after squeezing the soil

Clay
Smooth and sticky when wet
Can be shaped into a ball
Hand left dirty after squeezing the soil

Loam
Silky to the touch, neither coarse and gritty nor smooth and sticky
May shape into a ball but falls apart on leaving
Hand slightly dirty after squeezing the soil

37

Natural, factory-made and raw materials

Material is the stuff which things are made up of.

We often use the word material to mean fabric. Fabrics make up the clothes we wear and items like curtains, tablecloths and towels. Fabrics are just one kind of the many different materials in the world. A look at the labels on different fabrics will show that they are made from a very wide range of materials. Natural materials such as wool and cotton are often mixed together with factory-made materials like nylon and polyester.

Raw materials are the starting materials for making items in factories.

Wool ←
Cotton ← **Natural materials** found in the world and unchanged by people
Wood ←

Materials

Manufactured materials made in factories by people from raw materials
→ Metals
→ Plastics
→ Glass
→ Paper
→ Paint
→ Nylon

Raw material
Trees are natural resources. They take 30–100 years to grow.

Cut trees down, use large pieces like trunks and big branches

Manufacturing process
Finely divided wood is mixed with water, beaten up and made into pulp, then pressed into sheets

Finished product
Newspaper is cheap paper

Table and chair

Hardbacked books use high-quality paper

Metals: from ore to finished product

Some metals are found pure in the ground, not mixed with anything. These are rare. One such metal is gold which is usually found in small lumps called nuggets. Most gold is found in South Africa and western USA. Small amounts have been found in Wales and Cornwall.

Most metals are found in the ground as **ores**. An ore contains the metal mixed with other things. The ore of aluminium is bauxite. It is dug out of the Earth in mines.

Stage 1
Separate the metal from the other things

Stage 2
Manufacture products from the metal

Drinks cans made from aluminium can be recycled to reduce waste and save bauxite

Ceramics: from raw material to finished product

The raw material is clay from the ground

Shaped on potter's wheel or in a mould

Kiln: high-temperature oven where the clay is dried out. This is called **firing** the clay.

The word **ceramic** comes from the Greek word for pottery. Ceramics are among the oldest factory-made materials. Ceramic items are often found in excavations of ancient sites.

Glass

Glass is made by melting sand with limestone and sodium carbonate. This makes common glass as used in milk bottles, jam jars and wine bottles. Coloured glass is made by adding small amounts of impurities.

Bottles and vases are often made by glass-blowing. A lump of very hot soft glass, almost molten, is placed on the end of a long hollow tube. The glass-blower blows down the tube and shapes the glass object.

Plastics: just one of many products of oil

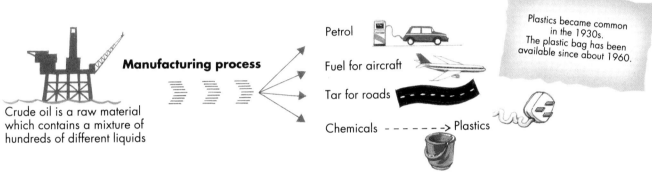

Crude oil is a raw material which contains a mixture of hundreds of different liquids

Manufacturing process

Petrol

Fuel for aircraft

Tar for roads

Chemicals - - - - - - -> Plastics

Plastics became common in the 1930s. The plastic bag has been available since about 1960.

Fibres

Fibres are hair-like strands. Different fibres have different properties. For example, cotton soaks up moisture and allows sweat to evaporate. This makes it a good material to wear in hot weather. Polyester does not soak up moisture like cotton, but it is hard-wearing.

This explains why shirts are often a mixture of the two, for example 65% polyester and 35% cotton. This mixture gives a hard-wearing material which is comfortable to wear in hot weather.

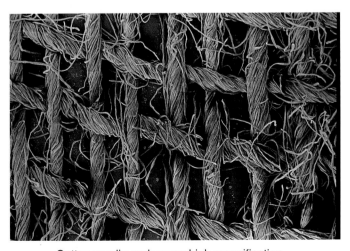

Cotton muslin under very high magnification

QUESTIONS

1. Why is wool called a natural material?

2. Why are newspapers made from cheap paper?

3. What name is given to small pieces of gold found in the ground?

4. What substance is lost when clay is fired?

5. From which language does the word ceramic come?

6. Suggest two disadvantages of a pure cotton shirt over a polyester/cotton one.

1. On your own copy, complete the nine horizontal words using the following clues (a) to (i). Then answer part (J).

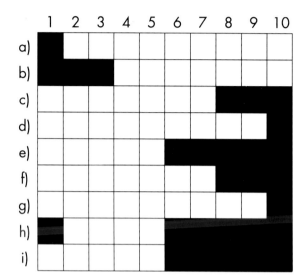

a) Bauxite is an ore of this metal.
b) Resources which are found in the world.
c) The material most buckets and biros are made from.
d) New things are made in manufacturing ____.
e) The material you are looking at.
f) Materials curtains, tablecloths and towels are made from.
g) The same as before (not changed).
h) Sheep's clothing.
i) You look through this to the world outside the classroom.
J) Now write down the word which appears in column 5 running from top to bottom.

2. Here are five types of material:

ceramics   fibres   glass   metals   plastics

Below are five definitions A to E. Match each definition to a material.

A Shiny, cold to the touch, bendable, smooth solids.
B Hard, brittle, dull, rough (unless painted), made from clay.
C Hard, smooth, brittle, see-through solids, cold to the touch.
D Smooth, warm to the touch, soft, bendable, solid, weak, sometimes see-through.
E Made from hair-like strands which are sometimes twisted or woven together, warm to the touch.

3. Knitting yarn comes in balls. Below are the labels from two different balls of yarn. Study them carefully and then answer the questions which follow.

a) Which natural materials are found in these yarns?
b) What percentage of natural material is found in A?
c) Which yarn has the highest percentage of acrylic fibre?
d) Which yarn contains metal? How do you know?
e) Give a reason why metal might be added.
f) Why are yarns a mixture of fibres?
g) Which yarn is better for summer wear? Why?
h) Why are pure wool jumpers warmer than synthetic jumpers?
i) Give two reasons why manufacturers give the fibre contents of the yarns.
J) Find a jumper at home. Look at the label. What fibres are in the jumper?

4. Some people talk of a 'plastics revolution'. They mean that plastics have taken over from other materials. Here is a table showing items now commonly made from plastic. On your own copy, complete the table.

Item	Older material	Advantage of plastic over older material
Dustbin		
Window frame		
Car bumper		
Carrier bag		
Suitcase		

5. Look at the drawing below of a modern kitchen, and then answer the questions which follow.
   a) Name three things in the drawing made mainly of metal.
   b) Name one thing made of glass.
   c) Name three things made from fibres.
   d) Name three things made of plastic.
   e) Name three things made mainly from a ceramic material.
   f) Why is it an advantage for the kitchen worktop to be smooth?
   g) Kitchen drawers can have plastic sides which fit into plastic runners. They can also have metal pieces on their sides which fit into metal runners. Which type of drawer runner would you expect to last longer and why?

   h) How should bottles of poisonous cleaning materials be kept in a kitchen? Why?
   i) Imagine you are carrying a pan of hot water around the kitchen in the picture. List all the hazards you can see.

Research

1. Find out how high-quality paper is made.

2. List between five and ten items at home made mainly from
   a) plastic b) metal c) fibres d) ceramic material.

Science Companions 1 © A Porter, M Wood, T Wood and Stanley Thornes (Publishers) Ltd, 1991

Strength

A material which will not easily change shape when you pull it is said to have a high **tensile strength**. One which will not easily squeeze or crush is said to have a good **compressive strength**.

Ropes have a high tensile strength. Nylon ropes are much stronger than the old ones made from hemp. Hemp is a natural material. It is a plant with strong fibres. Hemp ropes have to be thicker and heavier than nylon ones of the same strength.

Building bricks have a high compressive strength. One brick can support the weight of 40 000 others before being crushed. Concrete also has a high compressive strength, but it has a low tensile strength. Steel rods are used in concrete buildings to make reinforced beams. They increase the tensile strength of concrete.

Shape also plays an important part in strength. Many buildings contain I-shaped beams. These support floors between pillars. House roofs which slope are supported by wooden triangular shaped frames. The triangle is a very strong shape.

Flexibility

A material which is easy to bend is **flexible**. It needs both good tensile and good compressive strengths. You can see why in the sketch below.

As the material is bent, the side AB is first compressed and then stretched. Side CD is first stretched and then compressed.

Hardness

The **Mohs scale** is a scale of hardness. It was devised by Friedrich Mohs, a nineteenth-century German mineralogist (person who studies minerals). **Minerals** are substances which are mined from the Earth. Bauxite (aluminium ore) is a mineral. Minerals are **graded** according to which other minerals they will scratch. Lower-grade minerals can be scratched by those of higher grades. For example, quartz will scratch calcite but will be scratched by topaz.

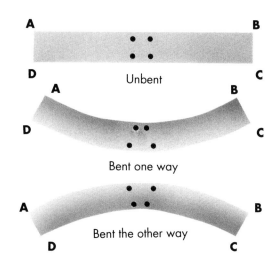

	Grade	Name of mineral	Everyday items
	10	Diamond	
	9	Corundum	
	8	Topaz	Knife sharpener
	7	Quartz	
Increasing hardness	6	Orthoclase feldspar	Penknife blade
	5	Apatite	
	4	Fluorite	Coin
	3	Calcite	
	2	Gypsum	Fingernail
	1	Talc	

The Mohs scale

Metals

Metals are strong, easily pressed into shapes and can give a smooth finish. They are ideal for car bodies. Styles can be changed regularly to encourage sales.

Stainless steel is used for kitchen sinks and cutlery as it can be cleaned easily.

Ceramics

Pots, bricks, paving stones and underground drainpipes are made of ceramics. Roofing tiles are made by heating together clay, sand and limestone. Designers of car and aircraft engines are trying to replace metal with ceramics. Ceramics will work at higher temperatures than metals so the engines would be more efficient.

These are also ceramics

Glass

In 1959 Pilkington Brothers invented the **float process** for making flat sheets of glass. Molten glass leaves a furnace at 1500 °C and floats on the surface of a bath of molten tin. The glass is then cooled slowly to prevent it cracking. Other processes make toughened glass for car and shop windows.

Coloured glass is called **stained glass**, and is usually seen in churches. Augsberg Cathedral in Bavaria, Germany, contains some of the oldest known stained glass, dating from AD 1050 to 1150.

Stained glass at Iffley Church, Oxford

Plastics

Leo Hendrich Baekeland (1863–1944) was a Belgian-American industrial chemist. He introduced **Bakelite** in 1909. This was the first widely used factory-made plastic. It is used as an electrical insulator in plugs and switches.

Bakelite hair dryer, 1930s

Old brown plugs and switches are made of Bakelite. The white ones used today are made from a urea-methanal resin.

Polythene is used in plastic bags and pipes, and for acid-resistant storage bottles. It was discovered by accident in 1933 at ICI by R. Gibson and E. Fawcett. Eighteen months later M. Perrin repeated the work, and only then was it realised how important the material might be.

Nylon

Wallace Carothers, an American working for the Du Pont Company, invented nylon. In 1937 he patented it for use in ladies' stockings. Until then, silk was the only suitable material for stockings. Silk is a very expensive natural fibre made by silkworms. The factory-made material rayon had failed earlier because it did not 'cling' properly and became baggy and wrinkled at the knees. During the Second World War, American servicemen spread the fame and advantages of 'nylons'.

QUESTIONS

1. Name two materials from which rope may be made.
2. Which rope material is preferred by climbers, and why?
3. Apatite is a grade 5 mineral on the Mohs scale. List some minerals which apatite will scratch.
4. Why is metal used in so many car bodies?
5. Where is some of the oldest stained glass?
6. Why was rayon a failure for ladies' stockings?

1. Complete this crossword on your own copy. It covers sections 3.1 and 3.2.

Across
1. The stuff which goes to make things (8).
4. A substance that contains a metal and other things (3).
6. Not bumpy (4).
9. If you heat things for too long they do this (4).
11. Eat, yesterday (3).
12. Liquid glass (6).
15. A blue material, mined in Wales, made into roofing 'tiles' (5).
16. An unforeseen problem, also to catch a thread in a jumper (4).
17. Pupils of a similar ability may be in these (4).
18. Raw unprocessed oil (5).
19. Precious stones (4).
20. A small computer or chip (5).
22. Not fast (4).
23. Hard-wearing, factory-made fabric (9).
25. Something which resists forces is this (6).
28. Not a fake (4).
29. The hardest mineral on Earth (7).
31. Opposite of 25 across (4).
33. See 24 down (9).
36. Not solids or gases (7).
38. A type of strength (7).
39. Naturally occurring solid substances (8).

Down
1. Substances found as 4 across (6).
2. A material in its natural state (3).
3. A common factory-made metal (9).
5. Used to be made of hemp, now usually made from 30 down (4).
6. Hair-like strands (6).
7. Mixture of gases all around us (3).
8. Material from clay (7).
10. Cheap paper (9).
13. Food is kept in these (4).
14. Small gold lumps (7).
18. Spies send messages in this form (4).
21. Small branch of a tree (4).
23. Most cars run on this today (6).
24. Glass is made by heating this (4) and 33 across (9).
26. Used for stirring. Made of glass (3).
27. Just made, not old (3).
30. Factory-made material, often used to make 5 down (5).
32. To increase by numbers (3).
34. More than one man (3).
35. First whole number after zero (3).
37. Sick, poorly (3).

2. Study the following drawings from *The Guardian* newspaper carefully. Read all the information at least twice before attempting to answer the questions which follow.

a) Why is the B2 bomber called a 'stealth' bomber?

b) What is the difference in wingspan between the two bombers?

c) What is the difference in crew numbers between the two bombers?

d) What radar echo is the B2 bomber claimed to have?

e) What type of materials give the B2 less radar echo?

f) Why is the B52 likely to be spotted by infra-red detectors?

g) Why is the B2 more likely to be a problem if there is a fire on board?

h) Why is chloro-fluoro-sulphonic acid used in the B2?

i) What is the problem associated with this acid?

J) Why does the B2 not have on-board radar?

B52 Stratofortress
263 B52 now in service with the US Air Force. Wingspan 185ft. Crew of six. Range 10,000 mls. Carries 12 Cruise missiles. Purpose: to destroy static targets with stand-off missiles.

The B52 is detected easily by radar at ranges of many hundreds of miles. External features on the B52 make it an ideal reflector of radar signals.

Why the B52 is easy to detect by radar...
1. Underwing fuel pods.
2. Eight underwing jet pods.
3. Infra-red detectors can locate heat from jet exhausts.
4. High altitude vapour trails attract visual attention.
5. The B52 is nearly all-metal construction.
6. Thick, blunt edges on wings.
7. Two underwing pods housing Cruise missiles.
8. Fuselage presents large surface areas head on to enemy radar.
9. B52's own search radar signals can be traced easily.
10. Huge tail stabiliser - nearly 500 square feet.
11. Distinctive fairing - called a 'strakelet' - attached to wing root for easy identification (in accordance with SALT treaty).

B2 Stealth Bomber
Purpose: to destroy mobile military targets with nuclear bombs.

Wingspan 175ft. Crew of two. Payload and range unknown.

The Stealth Bomber is planned to replace the ageing B52 and is designed to be nearly invisible to radar and other detection systems. Its radical design brings advantages and disadvantages.

FRONT VIEW OF STEALTH:
No blunt surfaces or blunt edges to reflect radar from front.(claimed to have radar echo of 'large bird')
Cockpit, fuselage and engines blended into wings.
Extensive use of non-metallic materials which gives less radar echo. No tail stabiliser.

Advantages:
1. Jet exhaust above wing-so less visible from below on Infra-red band.
2. Chloro-Fluoro-Sulphonic acid added to exhaust makes vapour trail invisible.
3. Windscreen coated with radar opaque material.
4. Jet turbo fans concealed.
5. Radar absorbing materials: layers arranged so that radar reflecting from inner layers cancels incoming radar in outer layers.

Disadvantages:
- Cost: Half a billion dollars for each Stealth bomber.
- Radical jet intake/exhaust design means slow speed.
- No external fuel pods mean fixed, limited range.
- Jets inside wing weaken structure. Fire - catastrophic!
- No tail stabiliser diminishes flight stability.
- CFS acid very corrosive to storage tanks & engines.
- Vapour trails still visible on ultra-violet bands.
- Still vulnerable to AWACS 'look-down' radar and to bi-static radar.
- Cannot use on-board radar to seek target or enemy will detect radar signals.

Peter Clarke

Try it yourself

1. How can one sheet of paper support a tin of beans?

Roll the paper into a tube and secure it with sticky tape. The tube will support a large tin of beans easily.

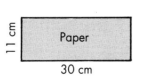

Sticky tape

5 cm

Paper
11 cm
30 cm

Beans

Beans
Paper tube

Try different types of paper and different sizes of tube to see how well they each support weights.

2. Paper is too flexible to bridge this gap. What shape can you make the paper to make it stronger?

cience Companions 1 © A Porter, M Wood, T Wood and Stanley Thornes (Publishers) Ltd, 1991

How a coffee filter works

A coffee filter machine uses several scientific ideas. This diagram shows how the water in the machine is **distilled**. This means that the water is first boiled to a gas and then condensed back into a liquid. You can also see how the coffee is separated from the coffee beans.

3 Some of the steam cools to below 100 °C. It then becomes liquid again (it **condenses**).

4 The hot condensed liquid water drips on to the crushed coffee beans.

Filter paper

5 The beans are crushed so that water can get inside. The water dissolves the colour and flavour of the coffee. The parts of the beans that do not dissolve stay in the filter.

Water

1 Cold water drips down on to an element.

6 The liquid coffee can pass through the holes in the filter paper. The pieces of coffee bean are too big and are trapped.

Element

2 The water boils to form steam, a gas. Steam forms at 100 °C.

Coffee

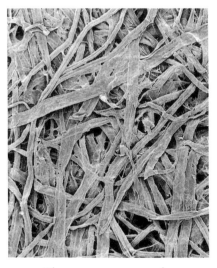

Filter paper as seen under a microscope

The paper that makes up the coffee filter looks like this under a microscope. You can see that it is made up of fibres that are locked together. These form holes or gaps that the coffee liquid can pass through. Tea bags are made of a similar paper. The tea leaves stay in the bag but the dissolved tea flavour and colour can pass through.

Using tap water in coffee filter machines can lead to fur or scale on the electric heater. Tap water is not pure water. It has many things dissolved in it. Some are added at the water treatment works, and others come from the rocks the water has passed through. Some rocks, like limestone, dissolve slowly in rainwater. If your water comes from an area with these rocks, it is called **hard** water. When you boil hard water in the heater, some of the dissolved substances get left behind and build up on the heater. This causes scaling or furring, which has to be removed from time to time. The problem can be avoided by putting water that is not hard in the machine.

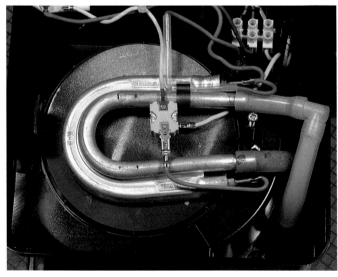

The water runs through this element and forms scale on the inside

Chromatography

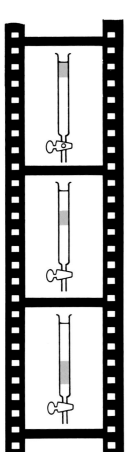

In 1903 the Russian biologist Michel Tswett was investigating the dyes that made plants green. He came up with a method that scientists still use today. The method is called **chromatography** and it is used to separate mixtures.

Tswett first separated the green colouring from leaves. He crushed the leaves up with a liquid that would dissolve the green colour. After filtering, he poured the coloured solution into a tall tube. The tube contained a special powder. This was soaked in the same liquid that dissolved the dye.

He let the liquid run through the powder by opening the tap at the bottom. He saw that the green colour separated into two coloured bands. This happens because the coloured solution contains different dyes. The dyes travel through the powder at different speeds. The dye that sticks to the powder best will travel down slowest.

It is easier for us to use paper than powder. Paper can soak up liquids, in the same way as the powder.

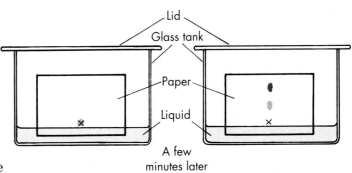

Lid
Glass tank
Paper
Liquid

A few minutes later

Water soaks upwards through the paper

It takes the colours with it

Smarties have coloured coatings on them. These coatings are not all single dyes. The table below shows some of the colours and the dyes they contain. The picture at the side is a **chromatogram** – a result of a chromatography experiment on a coffee coloured Smartie.

Colour of Smartie	Dyes used to make it
Orange	E110 sunset yellow E127 erythrosine (pink)
Green	E104 quinoline yellow Brilliant blue E110 sunset yellow
Pink	E127 erythrosine
Coffee	E104 quinoline yellow E110 sunset yellow E122 carmosine E127 erythrosine Brilliant blue

(The above information was supplied by Rowntrees UK)

QUESTIONS

1. What is water called when it is heated to a gas?

2. What does distillation mean?

3. Would it be a good idea to use sea water in a filter coffee machine? Why? Would the coffee made from it be drinkable?

4. Who invented chromatography?

5. Which of the Smartie colours opposite would produce a chromatogram with
   a) one colour
   b) two colours
   c) three colours?

1. In this puzzle there are seven clues. On your own copy, write the answers to the clues into the grid to the right. When you have done this, transfer the letters to the grid below. If you get the right letters in their correct spaces, a sentence will appear.

1. The opposite of sink.

1a	1b	1c	1d	1e

2. What is this?

2a	2b	2c	2d	2e	2f

3. A hot gas.

3a	3b	3c	3d	3e

4. Another word for grinding.

4a	4b	4c	4d	4e	4f	4g	4h

5. One way of drying liquids.

5a	5b	5c	5d	5e	5f	5g	5h	5i

6. What E122 is called.

6a	6b	6c	6d	6e	6f	6g	6h	6i

7. A way of purifying liquids.

7a	7b	7c	7d	7e	7f

1a	4f	7f	3b	4b	5c	1e	6g	1c	2c

3a	3c	5d	6b	6c	1d	7d	2e	7c

1e	4e	7b	2d	4h	3a

7d	4e	1d	3b

7a	7e	3a	4d	6e	7f	5b	3c

2a	5f	1c	6d

7d	4e	4f	2c	4h	4d

3b	4e	3d	1e

7a	5e

4g	1c	3b

2. Large blocks of marble are crushed to make chippings for road surfaces. The chippings need to be about 2 cm across. How could a supplier of chippings sort out the sizes so that customers will get the right size chipping?

3. Distillation can be used to separate the liquids in crude oil (petroleum). The liquids are called **fractions** of the petroleum and the process is called **fractional distillation**.
Each liquid boils over a different temperature

Science Companions 1 © A Porter, M Wood, T Wood and Stanley Thornes (Publishers) Ltd, 199

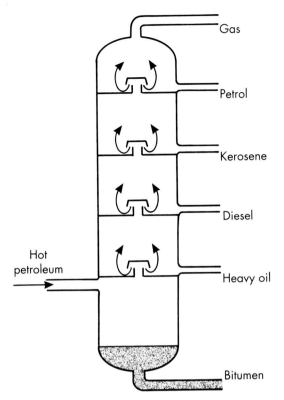

Gas

Petrol

Kerosene

Diesel

Hot petroleum

Heavy oil

Bitumen

range. The petroleum is heated to a gas and then passed into a large tower called a **fractionating tower**. Here the petroleum condenses in different layers of the tower. The easily condensed fractions (those with high boiling temperatures) collect at the bottom of the tower. At each stage up the tower the liquids get lighter and harder to condense. Any gases in the petroleum are collected at the top.

a) How many fractions of the petroleum are shown in the diagram?

b) Explain what is meant by the word 'condense'.

c) Choose two of the fractions and say what they are used for.

d) Which of the fractions has the lowest boiling temperature?

e) Which of the fractions is most likely to be a solid at room temperature?

4. Read this passage which tells you how baked beans are sorted and processed. Draw a picture of what you think the factory might look like and show what happens to the beans between arriving and leaving in their cans.

The beans used are haricot beans. When they arrive at the factory they need to be sorted. Any mouldy beans or foreign objects in the beans must be rejected before they are canned.

The beans are channelled past a beam of light. The light bounces off each bean in turn and enters a detector. This detector acts like an eye for a computer. If a bean is not as bright and shiny as it should be, a jet of air blows it off the conveyer belt. The computer is so fast it can sort 200 beans every second.

After sorting, the beans continue on the conveyor belt. They are heated in steam to soften their skins and then baked in a long oven. At the end of the oven the beans drop into empty cans and the correct amount of tomato sauce is added from another machine. Finally the cans are sealed and sterilised in steam before being labelled and packed in boxes.

Try it yourself

1. Try this way of separating a mixture of salt and pepper. Take one teaspoon of salt and one of pepper and mix them well. Pour the mixture into a glass of water and note what happens.

a) Write down what happens to the salt and the pepper.

b) If you left the glass to stand for a while what do you think would happen to the salt?

c) How could you recover separate samples of salt and pepper from the glass of water?

2. *Separating the colours in felt-tip pens*

| YOU WILL NEED THESE... straw felt pens | Cut out a strip of newspaper without any writing on it. Put a dot of felt pen near one end. | Pin the paper to the straw and hang it in the glass. Very carefully, pour in some water. The paper must dip in the water, but the dot must not. MEANWHILE... | While you are waiting to see what happens, think about these questions:
• Are any colours used in more than one pen?
• Does the size of dot make any difference?
• If so, what size of dot is best?
• What happens if you leave the experiment for a long time?
• What sort of paper works best? |

There's only one way to answer these... FIND OUT!

49

Acids

Acids are substances which have a sour taste. The word 'acid' means sour. These substances contain acids:

Substance	Name of acid
Soda water	Carbonic acid
Lemons, orange juice	Citric acid
Grapes	Tartaric acid
Vinegar	Ethanoic acid

All the acids shown above are safe – we can eat or drink them. However, in a laboratory there are dangerous acids. They can burn things. Their bottles carry a corrosive warning sign. You must wear safety glasses when handling them.
Three common laboratory acids are sulphuric acid, hydrochloric acid and nitric acid.

Alkalis

Alkalis are the 'opposites' of acids. Once again, many are found in the home.

Substance	Name of alkali
Ammonia	Ammonia solution
Oven cleaner	Sodium hydroxide
Toothpaste	Calcium carbonate
Milk of Magnesia	Magnesium hydroxide

Alkalis can dissolve your skin slightly, and produce a 'soapy' feeling. Two fingers coated with a solution of alkali feel slippery when rubbed together.

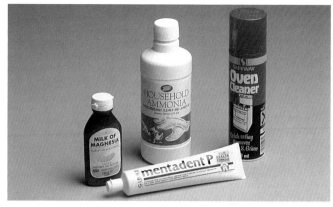

These are all alkalis

Soap is made by mixing together sodium hydroxide and a fat, and heating. Sodium hydroxide is a common laboratory alkali. It is a very strong alkali. An old name for solid sodium hydroxide is caustic soda. The word 'caustic' means burning. Alkali bottles also carry the corrosive warning sign.

Neutral solutions

Common salt is called sodium chloride by scientists. When it is dissolved in pure water it gives a solution which is **neutral**. This means that the solution is neither an acid nor an alkali. We can make neutral solutions by mixing together exactly the same amounts of acid and alkali.

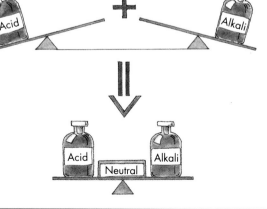

Indicators

Indicators are substances which turn different colours when placed in acid or alkali solutions. Some examples of laboratory indicators and their colours are shown opposite.

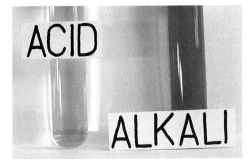

Phenolphthalein

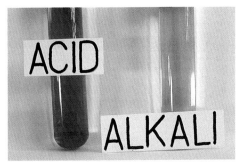

Methyl orange

Litmus is a form of lichen (plant life). It is a natural substance which is an indicator. There are many other natural indicators. Some fruit juices can be used such as blackcurrant jam, bilberries, strawberries and blackberries.

The pH scale

Knowing that a substance is an acid or an alkali is not always enough. Scientists often need to know how strong an acid or alkali is. There is a scale of numbers from 1 to 14 to measure this called the **pH scale**. 'pH' comes from the German meaning 'power of hydrogen'. All solutions which are acids contain hydrogen. (*Note*: not all solutions containing hydrogen are acids!)

We sometimes measure the strength of an acid or alkali using a **pH meter**. This has a **probe** which goes into the solution. Another way is to use **Universal Indicator** which is a mixture of several indicators. It changes colour many times over the full pH range. It is available as a solution or papers.

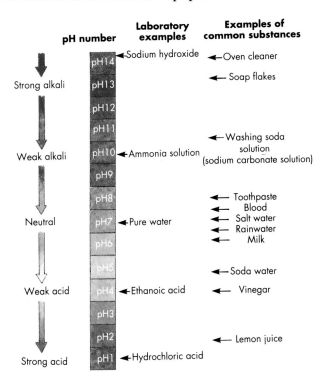

In the pH table shown above, toothpaste is given a pH of 8. In fact toothpastes can range from pH 7 to pH 10, depending upon their ingredients. The rainwater with pH 6.5 is unpolluted – acid rain can have a pH as low as 1.5 (see page 34).

QUESTIONS

1. What is the meaning of the word acid?

2. Give one safety measure taken when dealing with laboratory acids.

3. What is the meaning of the word caustic?

4. Which substance, often added to fish and chips, is neutral when dissolved in water?

5. From which language does the term 'pH' come, and what does it mean?

6. Name the indicator which is capable of showing the range of pH.

7. What is the approximate pH of blood?

8. Some sulphuric acid was spilled on to a laboratory bench. What steps should be taken to clear it up safely?

1. Study the following newspaper article, and then answer the questions which follow.

> ## WORLD NEWS   (20.3.90)
>
> ## Cashier hurt by robbers
>
> Joan Smith, head cashier at the Town Bank in Woodham, West Yorkshire, was badly burned in the face yesterday when two robbers threw acid at her. Detective Inspector Blenkinsop said that the robbers escaped without any money, in a stolen light blue Ford Escort. They are still at large and are believed to be dangerous. He said that the ammonia-like substance used by the robbers had caused severe facial burns to Miss Smith. He added that she was on the way to a complete recovery in Porterfield Hospital, where she was receiving expert attention.

a) Which bank did Joan Smith work for?

b) How many robbers raided the bank?

c) How much money did they steal?

d) Detective Inspector Blenkinsop said that an ammonia-like substance was used. Why is this probably an incorrect statement in view of a previous comment in the report?

e) What hazard label should be present as a warning on an acid bottle?

f) What is ammonia used for in the home?

2. In the letters below are hidden the names of seven acids mentioned in section 3.4. The names are printed left to right or read vertically from the top downwards. Write down the names of the acids.

C	O	U	T	A	B	L	E	R	I	C	O	T
R	I	G	T	H	O	B	T	O	R	I	C	U
T	H	Y	D	R	O	C	H	L	O	R	I	C
P	O	A	T	A	R	T	A	R	I	C	T	R
O	R	C	A	R	B	O	N	I	C	A	R	O
X	I	D	O	B	I	C	O	R	I	C	I	C
S	U	L	P	H	U	R	I	C	S	D	C	I
Y	C	N	I	T	R	I	C	H	J	K	P	Y

3. Below are the names of many substances which appear in the pH table in section 3.4. Replace the name with the pH it is given in the table and find the value of the question mark in each sum.

a) pH of sodium hydroxide − pH of soap flakes = ?

b) pH of ethanoic acid + ? = pH of toothpaste

c) ? + pH of hydrochloric acid = pH of toothpaste

d) pH of washing soda solution − ? = pH of vinegar

e) pH of oven cleaner − pH of pure water = ?

4. On your own copy, complete the seven horizontal words using the clues (a) to (g). Then answer part (h).

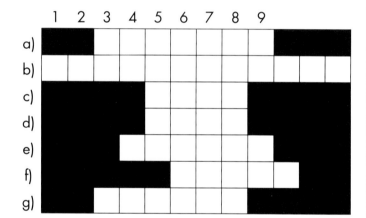

a) Ethanoic acid gives this liquid its taste.

b) The laboratory acid which suggests it contains hydrogen.

c) Can be delivered to your door in the morning, often added to tea or coffee.

d) This type of water is bubbly and contains carbonic acid.

e) If drinks are not sold in a can or carton, they are sold in a _____.

f) When you squeeze an orange a liquid comes out. It is called the _____ and contains citric acid.

g) These fruits contain tartaric acid.

h) Now find the word in column 8.

5. On your own copy, complete the blank spaces. Include any other indicators you have studied.

Indicator solution	Colour	
	In an acid	In an alkali
Litmus	Red	Blue
Phenolphthalein		
Methyl orange		

6. Some laboratory bottles have lost their labels. They all look the same. They are known to contain hydrochloric acid, ethanoic acid, pure water and sodium hydroxide solution. Suggest a method by which you could identify the contents of each bottle and so be able to label it correctly.

Try it yourself

1. *Make an indicator from red cabbage*
   Take an old glass or mug. Tear two red cabbage leaves into small pieces and place them in the glass or mug. Add warm water to just cover them, and stir. The water takes the colour out of the cabbage. The water goes purple and the leaves go almost white. Pour the coloured liquid into a separate container to use as an indicator.

Tear up   Warm (not boiling)

Now use your indicator solution to test various things at home to see if they are acidic or alkaline. An old egg cup will do as a 'test tube'. Add a little of the liquid under test, some water, then a few drops of red cabbage indicator. Read the labels on bottles first before using the contents. Do not use a bottle with a hazard warning label unless an adult is with you to watch.
Red cabbage indicator goes red in acids and green in alkalis.

2. Following the above recipe, how would you produce some red cabbage indicator paper? Try your method.

3. Ask your teacher for a few pieces of Universal Indicator paper to take home. Try testing different liquids and solutions of solids at home. Use an old cup or egg cup for the tests and ask an adult to help you. Read the labels on bottles first before using the contents. Do not use a bottle with a hazard warning label unless an adult is with you to watch.

Science Companions 1 © A Porter, M Wood, T Wood and Stanley Thornes (Publishers) Ltd, 1991

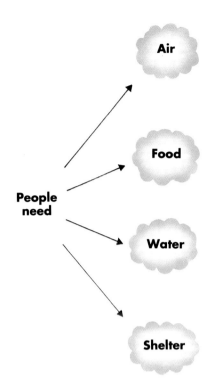

People need

Air
We need oxygen in the air to breathe.
We use oxygen from the air in industry.
We pollute the air with toxic gases
from chimneys.

Food
We eat food to give us energy.
We rear animals and grow plants to eat.

Water
We need water for drinking and washing.
We have to recycle water to use again.

Shelter
We need some form of shelter to keep
warm, dry and safe.
We use local materials to build shelters.

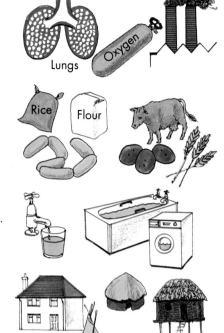

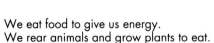

We need certain resources to live. The resources we need are food, shelter, air, water and warmth.

People have used the Earth's resources for their needs for thousands of years. In the past, there was a large supply of resources and people assumed that they would last forever, or that they could be replaced. For example, trees can grow again. The Earth's population is now so large that we demand more and more goods to be made, which uses up resources faster than before. The result is that the Earth's surface has been changed, and has been badly damaged in many places.

The changing face of the Earth

When we use resources from the Earth we change the way the Earth looks in a number of ways.

When resources are mined the workings are often ugly. When the mining is finished the land can be left scarred. Some companies clean up the land after they have changed it. Oil companies landscape the site after they have laid pipelines.

Installing a pipeline

After landscaping

The Norfolk Broads

The Norfolk Broads is an area of connected streams, lakes and marshes in Norfolk, England. In medieval times peat was taken from the ground and used for fuel. This left large holes in the ground. Later the sea level rose and flooded the land, leaving the rivers and lakes which we call the 'Broads'.

Peat is still cut in Britain. It is now used for gardening. Gardening is so popular that vast quantities are being cut. It is estimated that there are only 10 years' supply of peat left in Britain if it is cut at the present rate.

QUESTIONS

1. What do people need to live?
2. Why are the Earth's resources being exhausted so quickly?
3. Explain how the Norfolk Broads were formed.
4. What is the main use of peat today?
5. Why do people need a shelter?
6. Look at the photographs on these pages about how people have changed the environment. Explain how the environment has been changed in each case and why.

1. Study the plan below. It shows an area where the council plans to use the marshland as a landfill site to dispose of rubbish. Answer the questions which follow.

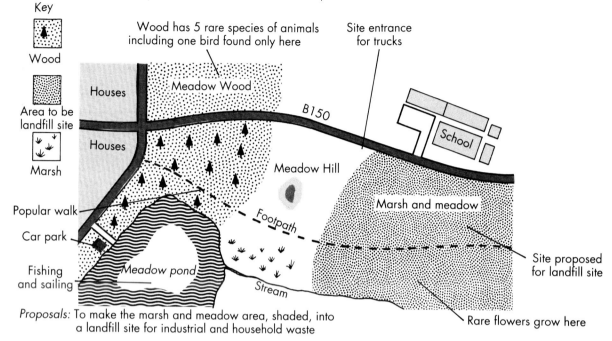

Key

Wood

Area to be landfill site

Marsh

Popular walk

Car park

Fishing and sailing

Wood has 5 rare species of animals including one bird found only here

Site entrance for trucks

Houses

Meadow Wood

Houses

B150

School

Meadow Hill

Meadow pond

Footpath

Marsh and meadow

Site proposed for landfill site

Stream

Rare flowers grow here

Proposals: To make the marsh and meadow area, shaded, into a landfill site for industrial and household waste

a) How will the appearance of the area change?

b) How will people be affected?

c) How will animals and plants be affected?

d) How might the health of people be affected?

e) Write a letter to your MP saying exactly how the landfill site will affect the area and your reasons why the proposals should be changed. Write another letter from the council saying why the site would benefit the area.

2. Read the following newspaper article about peat bogs, and then answer the questions which follow.

WORLD NEWS

(29.3.90)

Peat boom in Britain

Peat farming is big business in Britain. More and more people are gardening, and as a nation we buy tonnes of peat each year. Peat has many uses for gardeners, including for seed compost, potting plants and improving soil.

Peat comes from wetland bogs. It is cut out of the ground and sold in bags for gardeners. Peat bogs are covered with vegetation and are rich in rare plants and wildlife. A recent study showed that out of 130 original sites in Britain, only about 30 sites were left. Dr Moss from the Peat Institute said last night, 'When peat was cut for fuel the vegetation could regrow, but modern machines cut away all the peat and vegetation is never replaced'. Dr Moss went on to say that peat took 10 000 years to form and that there were only 90 000 hectares left in Britain. She said that there are substitutes like garden compost and animal slurry mixed with straw. A spokesman from Peato, a manufacturer of peat, said that they were leaving some peat behind and that vegetation will regrow.

a) Why is peat big business?

b) How is the peat being used?

c) Where does peat come from?

d) Why does cutting peat threaten nature?

e) What was peat used for in the past?

f) Why is peat no longer a popular fuel in Britain?

g) Why do modern methods of peat-cutting destroy vegetation?

h) How long did peat take to form?

i) How many hectares of peat are left?

j) What are the alternatives to peat?

Science Companions 1 © A Porter, M Wood, T Wood and Stanley Thornes (Publishers) Ltd, 1991

3. People do not always change the environment for the worse. 1990 was the 50th anniversary of National Parks in Britain. National Parks were created to protect beautiful areas, and to allow people to enjoy them.

The chart shows the approximate size of the National Parks in Britain and some of the animals and plants living there.

National Park	Size (square kilometres)	Animals/plants found
Dartmoor	950	Peat bogs, grass moors: foxes, deer, wild ponies, buzzards, owls
Northumberland	1000	Forest: grouse, dippers, wagtails, owls, roe deer
Brecon Beacons	1350	Foxes, badgers, otters, polecats, bats
Exmoor	670	Snipes, cuckoos, curlews, wild ponies
North York Moors	1440	Moorland: red grouse, foxes, stoats
Lake District	2300	Foxes, badgers, red deer, crested grebes, pike, perch
Snowdonia	2100	Foxes, badgers, pied catchers, fly catchers, otters, salmon
Pembroke Coast	590	Grey seals, foxes, badgers, razorbills, kitttiwakes, puffins
Peak District	1400	Woodcocks, sparrowhawks, owls, dippers, badgers

a) Why were National Parks created?
b) How do you think National Parks help the environment?
c) Using the figures in the table, draw a block graph (bar chart) to show the sizes of the parks.
d) Which is the largest National Park?
e) Name some animals found in this park.
f) Which is the smallest National Park?
g) Name some animals found in this park.

4. On your own copy, complete the six horizontal words using the following clues. Then find the word running from top to bottom which is something we need to live.

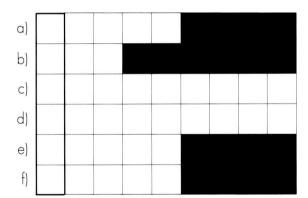

a) We drink and wash in this.
b) A gas we need.
c) Things we need to live.
d) Raw _____.
e) Too many are being cut down.
f) A form of shelter.
g) Now find the word running from top to bottom which is something we need to live.

5. Sort out the following mixed-up words. They are all raw materials.

a) AOCL
b) LIO
c) SAG
d) TEPA
e) ERTES
f) IAR

Research

Find out about your nearest National Park. Write about the scenery and activities that go on there.

You can find out about National Parks from the National Tourist Boards.

Try it yourself

1. Keep a record of which birds visit your garden or a park near you. Get your friends to do the same and then compare the results.

2. Find out about setting up bird boxes and tables. The Royal Society for the Protection of Birds can give you information.

3. Plant some wild flowers in your garden or school grounds.

Science Companions 1 © A Porter, M Wood, T Wood and Stanley Thornes (Publishers) Ltd, 1991

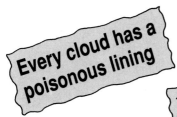

Every cloud has a poisonous lining

The North Sea is a rubbish tip

Toxic clouds kill frogs

10 more years of sewage dumping

Headlines like these can be seen in newspapers and magazines every day. They show how people have damaged the environment. People have been using land, food and resources from the Earth for many years and have ignored the effects this has. One effect that damages the Earth is **pollution**.

Pollution affects the land, seas, waterways and the air. Substances which harm the Earth are called **pollutants**. There are two types of pollutant. One type is **biodegradable**. These are things that can be broken down by nature, for example sewage and paper. The other type is called **non-biodegradable**. These things cannot be broken down by nature, so they build up in the environment, for example plastics and metals such as lead.

Pollution of the air

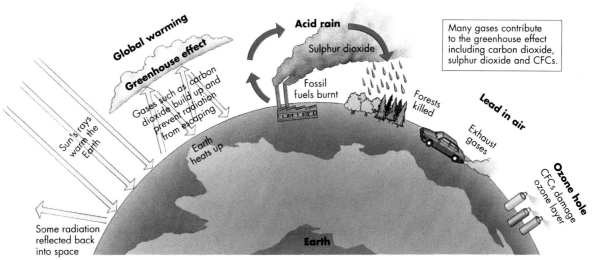

Many gases contribute to the greenhouse effect including carbon dioxide, sulphur dioxide and CFCs.

Acid rain
When fossil fuels are burnt they produce substances called oxides. Oxide of sulphur and nitrogen are released from tall chimneys into the atmosphere. The most damaging of these oxides is sulphur dioxide, a gas formed from burning coal. These oxides combine with water in the air to make dilute solutions of sulphuric acid and nitric acid. This makes **acid rain**. It falls back to Earth into the water cycle. Acid rain varies in its strength. Normal unpolluted rain has a pH of 6.5. The most acid rain has a pH of 1.5! Fish begin to die at levels below pH 4.5 and plants are damaged below pH 3.

The ozone layer
The ozone layer is a layer of gas about 12 kilometres above the Earth's surface. It protects the Earth from harmful ultraviolet rays from the Sun. A small hole has appeared in the ozone layer. The hole is thought to have formed because of the use of **CFCs** (chlorofluorocarbons). These are substances used in aerosol cans, fridges and in making plastic. A thinner ozone layer means that harmful ultraviolet rays can reach the Earth's surface, and overexposure to these rays can cause skin cancer.

Global warming

CFCs and carbon dioxide form a layer of gas in the atmosphere around the Earth. They stop the heat escaping from the Earth. As a result, the Earth warms up. This is called the **greenhouse effect** and some scientists believe it is changing the Earth's climate. In the last 100 years, the Earth has warmed up by half a degree Celsius.

Cars

Thousands of tonnes of lead are released into the air from car exhausts each year. Lead is added to petrol to improve combustion. Lead is most damaging to children living in cities where there are high lead levels in the air. Lead poisoning can cause brain damage. Most new cars can run on unleaded petrol or be converted to do so. In the future, lead pollution should be less of a problem.

Pollution of the land

Homes, factories, schools and shops all produce waste which is thrown away. On average in Britain we each throw away 160 kg of rubbish every year. Most household rubbish is paper but we also throw away plastics, food, metals and glass. Rubbish which is non-biodegradable may lie around for hundreds of years, causing eyesores and health problems.

How long does litter linger?

Cigarettes	1 to 5 years
Orange peel	2 years
Plastic bags	10 to 20 years
Nylon fabric	30 to 40 years
Tin cans	50 years
Ring pulls	80 to 100 years
Six-pack holders	100 years
Glass bottles	1 000 000 years

Pollution of the sea and waterways

Industrial waste and raw sewage are dumped into the seas. The North Sea is Europe's dirtiest sea from dumping. Chemicals from industry are put into rivers and waterways. Household chemicals are put down the drain and end up in the water cycle.

Some toxic chemicals in our waterways are shown in the table below.

Chemical	Found in	Effects
Phosphates Chemicals from nature essential for life	Detergents, fertilisers, household cleaners, industrial waste	If too much gets into the rivers lots of algae grow. These stop sunlight getting to plants, killing them and fish
Dioxins Chemicals produced when bleach is used	Paper products, e.g. nappies, toilet paper	Kill plants and animals in rivers and seas
Heavy metals Poisonous metals like lead, mercury and cadmium	Used in industry and for making batteries	Kill plants and animals, create 'dead' lakes

Umbrellas up, lads, raw sewage ahead!

QUESTIONS

1. What do we call damage to the Earth?

2. What are the two types of pollutant?

3. How is sulphur dioxide formed?

4. What does the ozone layer do?

5. Make two lists, one of biodegradable rubbish and one of non-biodegradable rubbish.

6. How do harmful chemicals get into the water cycle?

1. Copy the table below and write the substances under the correct heading.

plastic bottles   wood
cardboard boxes   tea-bags
woollen jumper   tin cans
Perspex box   grass cuttings
sewage   acrylic jumper
leaves   lead
crisp bag   newspaper
tights   glass bottle
compost   plastic carrier bag

Biodegradable	Non-biodegradable

2. Match the words with the meanings.

Words
environment   biodegradable   pollutant
resource   toxic   non-biodegradable

Meanings

a) A supply of plants, animals, fuels, minerals or raw materials found in an area.

b) A poisonous substance produced by an animal, plant or chemical reaction is this.

c) The conditions around a living thing which affect the way it lives.

d) A substance which can be broken down by nature.

e) Substances which harm the Earth and living things.

f) A substance which cannot be broken down by nature.

3. *A short poem*

Litter, litter everywhere.
You see it here, you see it there.
On the streets and in the park.
You can even see it in the dark.
Humans are the ones to blame,
animals are at risk, it's such a shame.
Look after the Earth, please try;
if you do not, it will surely die.

Write your own poem about litter or pollution. Write it out on a large sheet of paper and pin it up around the school.

4. Unscramble the words downwards to find another word for harmful substances in the top line.

U	E	L	N	A	O	D	E	I
I	N	D	A	D	X	S	D	R
O	O	A	D	D	T	U	O	T
P	Z	E	L	E	I	I	X	I
S	O			E	C	N	I	N
O				L		T	S	C
N				N		R		
O				U		Y		
S								

5. *A day in the life of the Bloggs family*

A The Bloggs set out for a day at the seaside. They stop for petrol.

B On the way, Dad dumps some rubbish in a ditch, an old chair, a petrol can without a lid and some garden rubbish including old bottles of garden sprays.

C A stop for a snack. They eat their burgers packed in foam trays outside.

D At the beach they have a huge picnic including pop, crisps, fish and chips and fruit. There is no bin on the beach.

For each of the pictures A to D, list the ways the Bloggs family pollute the air, land and water and how they can put it right.

6. *True or false?*
Read each of the following statements about pollution, then write out those which are true.
a) When fossil fuels are burnt they produce substances called oxides.
b) The pH of unpolluted rain is 3.0.
c) The ozone layer is a hole above the Earth.
d) The greenhouse effect is cooling down the Earth.
e) A person in Britain throws away about 160 kg of rubbish a year.
f) Lead is added to petrol to improve combustion.
g) Phosphates are chemicals in nature essential to life.
h) Lead, mercury and cadmium are all poisonous metals.

7. The diagram shows an open tip above a lake.

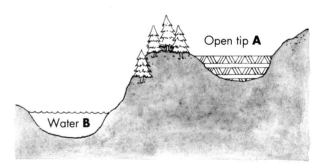

Copy the diagram, and using words and arrows explain how chemicals from the tip (A) get in the water (B). Use these words to help you:

leach rain falls soaks runs water table
soil washed lake dissolves

The Earth has suffered a great deal of pollution. There are ways of preventing pollution, but they take time to set up and are expensive.

Governments and local councils can pass laws to:

- stop liquid industrial waste being dumped
- stop raw sewage being dumped
- stop harmful gases being released by factories and power stations
- increase the number of environmental officers
- prosecute people who break pollution laws.

What needs doing?

Some of the following things are being done, but we need to do more.

On land

Damaged forests can be replanted but this is expensive and trees take years to grow. Litter can be cleaned up. About 90% of litter can be recycled. Checks need to be made on the amount of fertilisers put on to the land. Too much fertiliser leaches into rivers and pollutes them.

Effects of acid rain on a forest in Czechoslovakia

In seas

A lot of pollution in seas results from accidents where toxic substances or oil are spilled. Oil tankers wash out their tanks at sea. This accounts for about 20% of oil pollution. Some countries have stopped dumping raw sewage into seas, but others still do this.

On waterways and rivers

Lime can be added to acid lakes to make them less acid, but it has to be added repeatedly as it does not last. All toxic industrial chemicals released into rivers should be banned. Phosphate-free detergents can help.

Crude oil spill off the Devon coast

In the air

The Clean Air Act of 1956 stopped black smoke being released into the air. Before this there were **smogs** in Britain – mixtures of smoke and fog. Filters can be fitted to chimneys to trap dust, and power stations can stop releasing poisonous gases (see next page). Most modern cars can run on lead-free petrol already or can be converted to do so.

What can industry do?

One of the worst pollutants in Britain is acid rain. British power stations produce acid rain because they make electricity by burning coal. Coal contains sulphur which forms the gas sulphur dioxide when burnt. Power stations can reduce sulphur dioxide by

- burning an alternative fuel like gas
- burning coal which contains less sulphur

- taking out the sulphur before burning the coal
- converting power stations so they can remove sulphur dioxide from the gases they release.

Drax power station in Yorkshire, the largest in Europe, is being fitted with an **FGD plant**. This will reduce the sulphur dioxide being released. The FGD at Drax and another at Fiddlers Ferry in Cheshire will reduce the total sulphur dioxide released in the air from Britain's power stations by 15%.

FGD stands for **flue gas desulphurisation**. This is a process which removes 90% of the sulphur dioxide from the gases released. At Drax the limestone/gypsum method is being used. Here limestone slurry washes out the sulphur dioxide and produces a substance called gypsum. This can be used to make plaster. Drax will use about 600 000 tonnes of limestone a year and produce one million tonnes of gypsum. The limestone used will not come from Britain's National Parks.

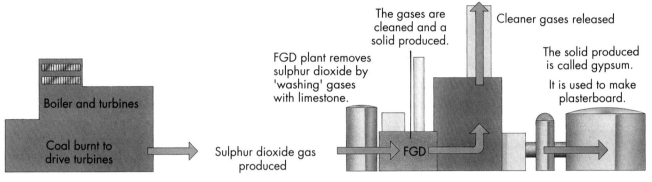

Boiler and turbines

Coal burnt to drive turbines

Sulphur dioxide gas produced

FGD plant removes sulphur dioxide by 'washing' gases with limestone.

The gases are cleaned and a solid produced.

Gases with 90% of sulphur dioxide removed

Cleaner gases released

The solid produced is called gypsum.

It is used to make plasterboard.

FGD

What can we do?

Use CFC-free aerosols.

Look for the ozone friendly symbol.

Try to buy CFC-free packaging like foam trays and plastic bags.

Use phosphate-free detergents and bleaches.

Change to organic gardening.

Change to unleaded petrol.

Get rid of waste carefully and report pollution.

Give up smoking or do not start.

Join a group to stop pollution.

Take paper and bottles to recycling bins.

Look for recycled labels on products.

Set up birdboxes and tables for birds and other wildlife.

Buy free-range eggs and meat.

QUESTIONS

1. Why has it taken so long for governments to act on pollution?

2. What causes about 20% of all pollution in seas?

3. How was smog stopped in Britain?

4. Give two ways of stopping lead pollution in the air.

5. What is Europe's largest power station called?

6. How can power stations reduce the sulphur dioxide released?

7. What does FGD stand for?

8. How does an FGD plant reduce sulphur dioxide?

9. Which useful substance is made using the FGD system?

1. **Catalytic converters** can be fitted to car exhausts. They reduce toxic gases released by exhausts. Read the newspaper article opposite, and answer the questions which follow.

   a) Name the three gases entering the catalytic converter from the car engine.
   b) Name the gases leaving the catalytic converter.
   c) What is the housing of the converter made of?
   d) Name the two metals which line the ceramic body.
   e) Which country fits catalytic converters to all new cars?
   f) What is the main 'greenhouse' gas?
   g) Which gas contributes to acid rain?
   h) Which substances irritate the lungs?
   i) What are noxious gases?
   j) What sort of fuel must be used with a catalytic converter?

2. Write out each word and the word in brackets which is closest to its meaning. One has been done for you.

   e.g. REDUCE   (make less) (increase) (small)
   Answer: Reduce is the same as *make less*

   a) TOXIC   (edible) (poisonous) (pleasant)

   b) COMBUSTION   (burning) (mixing up) (pollution)

   c) RAW   (cooked) (untreated) (unnatural)

   d) LEACHED   (washed away) (bleached) (blocked)

   e) CONVERTED   (separated) (changed) (purified)

   f) ALTERNATIVE   (different) (useful) (changing)

   g) LEVELS   (heights) (amounts) (stages)

   h) REMOVE   (take out) (replace) (travel)

   i) EMITTED   (given out) (shouting) (burnt)

   j) FILTERED   (smoothed) (cleaned) (untreated)

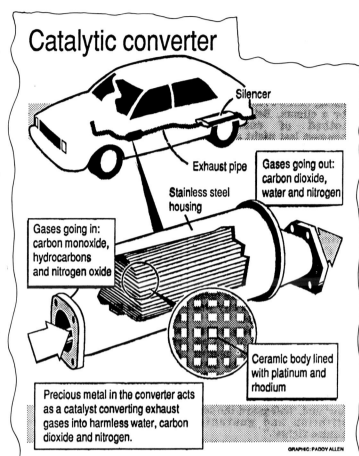

Catalytic converter

Silencer

Exhaust pipe

Gases going out: carbon dioxide, water and nitrogen

Stainless steel housing

Gases going in: carbon monoxide, hydrocarbons and nitrogen oxide

Ceramic body lined with platinum and rhodium

Precious metal in the converter acts as a catalyst converting exhaust gases into harmless water, carbon dioxide and nitrogen.

GRAPHIC: PADDY ALLEN

THE catalytic converter is the only device which can cut car exhaust emissions by up to 90 per cent to meet the stringent standards demanded in Europe but threatened by UK opposition, *writes James Erlichman.*

In the United States all new cars have been fitted with a "cat" since 1983.

A car engine belches out four main chemical pollutants which put at risk human health and the environment. They are carbon dioxide, the main "greenhouse gas"; nitrogen oxides, contributing to acid rain and the "greenhouse" effect; carbon monoxide, human toxin which adds to the "green-house" effect, and hydrocarbons, which irritate the lungs.

A full "three-way" catalytic converter fitted to the exhaust cuts carbon dioxide emissions by nearly 20 per cent and changes most of the other harmful gases into harmless water and nitrogen.

The noxious gases are forced to pass through the ceramic honeycomb structure of the converter coated with a thin layer of platinum and other precious metals.

Catalytic converters, costing about £50, must run on un-leaded fuel since lead ruins platinum's active properties. Other essential parts take the cost to up to £400.

3. The following sequences represent activities which cause pollution. The boxes in columns 1, 2 and 3 show the effects of pollution and how to clean it up. Unfortunately these boxes have been mixed up in each column. Redraw each sequence in the correct order.

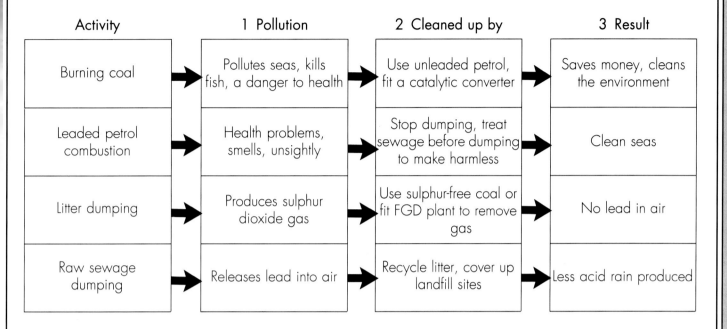

Activity	1 Pollution	2 Cleaned up by	3 Result
Burning coal	Pollutes seas, kills fish, a danger to health	Use unleaded petrol, fit a catalytic converter	Saves money, cleans the environment
Leaded petrol combustion	Health problems, smells, unsightly	Stop dumping, treat sewage before dumping to make harmless	Clean seas
Litter dumping	Produces sulphur dioxide gas	Use sulphur-free coal or fit FGD plant to remove gas	No lead in air
Raw sewage dumping	Releases lead into air	Recycle litter, cover up landfill sites	Less acid rain produced

4. *Word maze*

The answers to these questions are found in the grid below. On your own copy, cross the letters off for each answer. The next answer starts on an adjacent square to the last letter of the previous answer. You can go up, down, left or right but not diagonally. The first one has been done for you. When you have finished there will be one letter that is not crossed off. Find the letter.

a) Waste material (7).   RUBBISH
b) Use again (7).
c) The 'world around us' (11).
d) Pure and unpolluted (5).
e) A greenhouse gas (6, 7).
f) A metal that be recycled (9).
g) Pollution caused by burning fossil fuels (4, 4.)
h) These produce most acid rain (5, 7).
i) Another word for toxic (9).
J) What is happening to waste on land? (7)
k) Pollution dumped in the sea (6).
l) Places where waste is left (4).
m) Now find the one letter which is not crossed off.

START ➤

R	U	B	D	R	N	P	O	W	E
O	R	B	I	A	I	Q	S	P	R
N	I	I	C	A	M	U	I	I	S
M	V	S	H	R	E	C	N	T	T
E	N	E	E	L	C	Y	I	E	A
N	T	C	E	A	L	U	M	G	T
A	E	L	D	U	S	I	N	A	I
N	C	A	I	O	D	P	G	W	O
O	B	R	X	N	U	M	S	E	N
N	D	I	O	O	S	I	O	P	S

Try it yourself

Take some Universal Indicator paper home and try to find the pH of your rainwater. You can test it as it falls on to the paper, or you can collect it in a clean container and test it later. (Details of Universal Indicator paper are in section 3.4.)

cience Companions 1 © A Porter, M Wood, T Wood and Stanley Thornes (Publishers) Ltd, 1991

The waste we throw away contains valuable resources which can be used again. **Recycling** means making new products from waste materials.

Things that cannot be recycled are made of **non-renewable resources**. This means that once used, they cannot be used again. Fuels like coal, oil and gas are non-renewable. About 90% of household or domestic waste can be recycled.

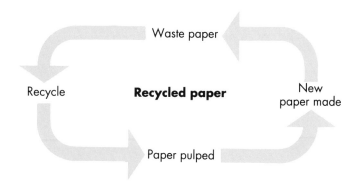

Waste paper → New paper made → Paper pulped → Recycle → **Recycled paper**

What's in a load of rubbish?

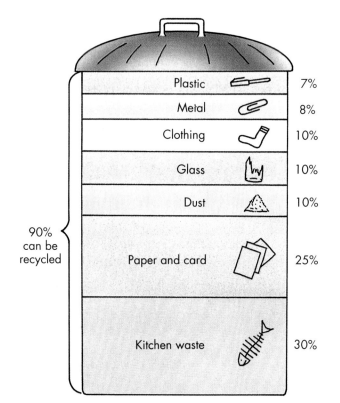

Plastic	7%
Metal	8%
Clothing	10%
Glass	10%
Dust	10%
Paper and card	25%
Kitchen waste	30%

90% can be recycled

What happens to our waste?

Most household waste is put into holes in the ground or on to tips. A landfill site is a hole in the ground which is filled with rubbish and then used to build on when the hole is full. A rubbish tip, where rubbish is left on top of the ground, is an eyesore and can be a health risk.

When tips and landfill sites are covered up they can still cause problems. When waste rots it gives off gases such as carbon dioxide and methane. These gases help to increase the greenhouse effect. Toxic chemicals from waste leach into the ground and get into the water cycle. If rubbish is burnt, it produces toxic gases which increase acid rain.

People also leave rubbish where it is a danger to health and animals.

Saving resources ⬜ ⬜ ⬜ ⬜

If we recycle rubbish it saves valuable new resources, money and energy.

Recycle it and

Save money
Save resources
Conserve the environment
Reduce waste
Help charities
Create employment

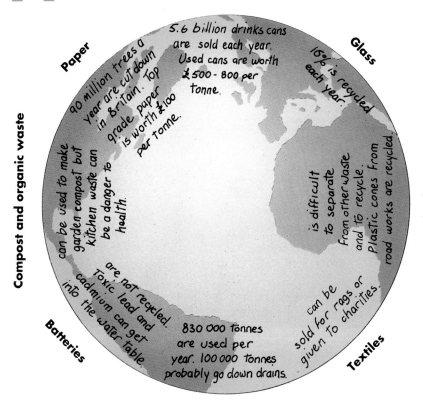

Aluminium

5.6 billion drinks cans are sold each year. Used cans are worth £500 - 800 per tonne.

Paper

90 million trees a year are cut down in Britain. Top grade paper is worth £100 per tonne.

Glass

18% is recycled each year.

Plastic

is difficult to separate from other waste and to recycle. Plastic cones from road works are recycled.

Compost and organic waste

can be used to make garden compost but kitchen waste can be a danger to health.

Batteries

are not recycled. Toxic lead and cadmium can get into the water table.

Car oil

830 000 tonnes are used per year. 100 000 tonnes probably go down drains.

Textiles

can be sold for rags or given to charities.

It takes a lot less energy to make new products from recycled materials than to make them from raw materials.

Bottle tops
Cans
Kitchen foil
Drinks cans

20 times as much energy to make new aluminium compared with melting down aluminium and recycling it

Stationery
Toilet rolls
Newspaper

Twice as much energy to make new paper from wood compared with recycling used paper

Bottles

Recycling one tonne of glass saves 30 gallons of oil

⬜ ⬜ Things we can do each day ⬜ ⬜

- Return milk bottles.
- Take glass bottles to bottle banks.
- Re-use plastic carrier bags.
- Pick up litter or report it to the council.
- Buy the largest packet you can afford in supermarkets to save packaging and petrol.
- Try to choose recycled paper products.
- Give old clothes to charities and rag merchants.
- Look for can skips or an aluminium collection scheme in your area.
- Buy a recycling directory and find out where to take rubbish for recycling.

QUESTIONS

1. What does recycling mean?
2. What is a non-renewable resource?
3. How is rubbish a danger when left in tips?
4. Make a list of things that can be recycled.
5. Why is it cheaper to recycle materials than to make new ones?

1. *Recycle it: quiz*
   Think about how you and your family get rid of rubbish. On your own copy,
   answer the questions and give yourself marks for each.

   Section A Score: never = 3, sometimes = 2,
   often = 0

   a) Do you throw litter on the street? ____
   b) Do you drink canned drinks? ____
   c) Do you use items packaged in plastic? ____
   d) If someone at home changes the car oil, does it go down the drain? ____
   e) Shops often give away plastic bags. Do you accept them? ____
   f) Do you throw old clothes in the dustbin? ____

   Score ____

   Section B Score: always = 3, sometimes = 2,
   often = 0

   g) Do you take bottles to bottle banks? ____
   h) Do you have a compost heap in the garden? ____
   i) Do you buy items made from recycled paper? ____
   J) Do you take litter home if there is no bin? ____
   k) Do you take newspapers to collecting bins? ____

   Score ____

   Total score: 0–10 Try to do more. 11–22 Quite good, keep it up. 23+ Excellent.

2. Solve the clues to find the message. Fill the answers in on your own copy.
   The first letter of each word or picture fits into the message. There are 26
   letters to find. Each goes in order as shown below.

   1 2 3 4 5 6 7   8 9   10   11 12 13 14 15 16 17 18   19 20 21 22 23 24 25 26

Clues

1. Making new products from waste. _ _ _ Y _ _ _ _ _

2. Litter on streets looks _ _ S _ _ _ _ _ _.

3.

4.

5. Objects. _ T _ _ _

6. We must _ _ V _ resources.

7. Most _ _ _ _ _ _ _ _ D rubbish is put on tips.

8. _ T takes less energy to recycle materials.

9.

10. A valuable recycled metal. _ L _ _ _ _ _ _ _

11. The amount of space taken up. _ _ _ _ _ E

12.

13. A _ _ _ D of old rubbish.

14. Not used means _ _ U _ _ _.

15. _ _ _ _ T 90% of rubbish can be recycled.

Science Companions 1 © A Porter, M Wood, T Wood and Stanley Thornes (Publishers) Ltd, 199

16.

17. Not more. _ _ _ S

18. Not full. _ _ _ _ Y

19.

20. Walking is good _ X _ _ _ _ _ _ .

21. Shops _ _ L _ things to buy.

22. Not new. _ L _

23. Not on the surface. _ N _ _ _

24.

25. Garden _ _ _ P _ _ _ can be made from kitchen waste.

26. At last you have reached the _ _ D.

---

3. *Recycling aluminium*

Read the passage about aluminium. On your own copy, fill in the missing words from the list opposite.

Millions of drinks cans are sold in Britain each year. Half of these cans are made of _____. You can find out if a can is aluminium or not by using a magnet. Aluminium is a non-ferrous metal – it is not _____, so a magnet will not _____ to its side.

    It is cheaper to _____ aluminium metal because it takes 95% less _____ than producing metal from _____. Recycling aluminium saves _____ and helps the _____ because it reduces the amount of _____ buried in the ground. Drinks cans make up about 10% of _____ waste. Aluminium cans are _____ about 50p per kilogram.

| household |
| environment |
| ore |
| litter |
| recycle |
| stick |
| magnetic |
| aluminium |
| energy |
| resources |
| worth |

---

4. Which object would go into which bin for recycling?

Pictures

A
B
C
D
E
F
G
H
I
J

Bins

1	2	3	4	5	6
C O M P O S T	B O T T L E S	P A P E R	A L U M I N I U M	N O N B I O D E G R A D A B L E	C L O T H I N G

5. On your own copy, fill in the words to complete the grid. (*Hint:* count the letters.)

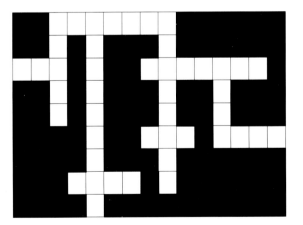

Words				
burn	tip	bottles	dump	clothing
plastic	paper	lead	oil	aluminium

Science Companions 1 © A Porter, M Wood, T Wood and Stanley Thornes (Publishers) Ltd, 1991

A **fuel** is a substance that has energy 'locked up' in it. People have learned to 'unlock' this energy and use it for heating, cooking and also for industry and transport.

Most of the fuels we use are **non-renewable** – once used, they cannot be replaced. For example, there are limited amounts of oil, gas and coal which will eventually run out. Because of this, we need to search for new fuels.

Most of our fuels are **fossil fuels**. They were made a long time ago when the remains of plants and animals became covered by mud. When the mud turned to rock, it trapped the remains. They changed under the pressure of the rock and the heat from inside the Earth.

Oil and gas

Oil and gas were formed millions of years ago from the plant and animal life that lived in the sea. Oil forms so slowly that we will use it up long before any more can be made.

1. Dead sea animals and plants drift to the sea bed and become covered in mud.

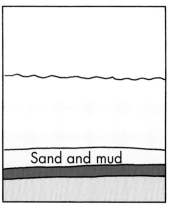

2. Layers of sand and mud build up on top. This squeezes the remains of the plants and animals.

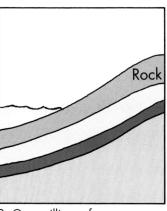

3. Over millions of years more rock forms on top. The mud and remains are squeezed so hard they make a rock called shale.

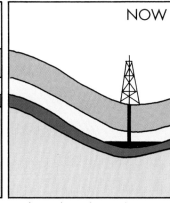

4. The rocks in the Earth move slowly. What was the sea bed may become land. Oil and gas form where the shale is trapped below hard rock.

To bring the fuel to the surface, the rocks above the oil and gas are drilled through. After cleaning, the gas can be used directly as a fuel. Most of the gas we use in homes and school laboratories is **North-Sea gas**.

The oil that comes up is known as **crude oil** or **petroleum**. It is a mixture of many different liquids. These liquids each have many uses. The petroleum is separated into the different liquids, which are called **fractions** of the petroleum. The process of separation is called **fractional distillation**, and it happens at an oil refinery. The petroleum is heated and the different liquids can be collected because they have different boiling temperatures.

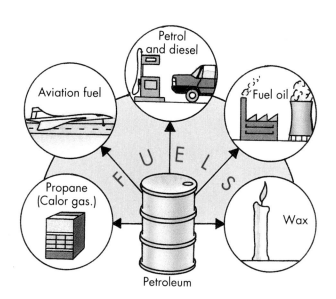

Petrol and diesel
Aviation fuel
Fuel oil
Propane (Calor gas.)
Wax
Petroleum

Coal

Like oil and gas, coal was formed from living things, millions of years ago. Coal is made mainly from plants that grew in huge fern forests when dinosaurs lived on the Earth. It is possible to find fossils of the ferns in lumps of coal.

Most of the coal mined in the UK is used in power stations to make electricity. Coal is a fuel that burns to form thick smoke. The Clean Air Act of 1956 made it illegal for people to burn coal in smoke-free zones (see section 4.3). They have to use a smokeless fuel such as coke.

Peat

Peat is formed in a similar way to coal, under moss in areas of bogland. It is wetter than coal and has to be dried out before it can be burned. In Ireland, a power station has been built to burn peat fuel. Once again, peat is a limited resource which is not quickly renewable (see section 4.1).

Digging peat

Hydrogen

This is the fuel that may one day be used in nuclear fusion power stations. Today it is used in a different way. The hydrogen is burned in air. It combines with oxygen to form only one product – water. A lot of heat is given out and there is no pollution. It is used as a rocket fuel in the space shuttle, where it is burned with pure oxygen.

The main disadvantage is that hydrogen is explosive. Although it can be made to burn safely, it has caused many accidents.

The explosion that destroyed the space shuttle *Challenger*, killing all seven crew, on 28 January 1986

Nuclear fuels

There are certain metals whose atoms are unstable. When the atoms break up they release a lot of **nuclear energy**. The process is called **nuclear fission**. The most common source of nuclear energy is uranium.

People thought nuclear fuels would be the answer to the fossil fuel shortage. However, the major problem of what to do with the radioactive waste has still not been solved. The energy is not as cheap as was first hoped because it costs a lot of money to build the power stations.

Scientists are working on another source of nuclear energy – from **nuclear fusion**. Two small atoms are forced to merge together to form a new atom. When this happens a lot of energy is given out. If the process can be made to work it should provide cheaper energy and a cleaner environment.

QUESTIONS

1. What fuels are made from petroleum?

2. Where does much of the gas that is used in the UK come from?

3. Why do we call oil, gas and coal fossil fuels?

4. How is the smokeless fuel called coke made?

5. How is uranium different from the other fuels mentioned?

6. Write down some advantages of using hydrogen as a fuel, and one disadvantage.

1. *Solar energy*

The Sun's heat can warm up water pipes that are painted black so they absorb heat

Sunlight can be changed into electricity using a solar panel

Sunlight can be changed into plant material like wood and used as a fuel or eaten by an animal

There is one fuel that is free and will last for millions of years. It is not found on Earth, but in the Sun. We will probably use the energy that reaches the Earth from the Sun a lot more in the future.

The Sun is a nuclear fusion reactor, 150 million km away. Hydrogen atoms are fused together in the Sun. It is possible to change sunlight into other forms of energy.

a) What fuel does the Sun use?
b) How does nuclear fusion work?
c) Why will solar energy last millions of years?
d) Why are water pipes in solar panels painted black?
e) What other devices use solar cells?
f) What stops solar cells being more widely used?
g) How can we use the energy that is stored in plants?

2.

WORLD NEWS　　(3.3.89)

Fatal blast in Russia

Four men were killed and six others were injured in an explosion at a Russian gas refinery station yesterday. The explosion was caused by propane gas at the Minnibayevsky gas refinery, 800 km east of Moscow. The blast smashed windows nearly 1 km away. The pipelines leading from the gas distillation plant were shut off immediately after the accident.

Read the newspaper article and answer the questions below.
a) Which fuel caused the explosion?
b) What do we use this fuel for in the UK?
c) Where does the fuel come from?
d) What happens in a refinery?
e) Why were the pipelines shut off?
f) What does distillation mean? (Look it up in the index if you do not know.)

3. This chart shows fuels that are used in the world.

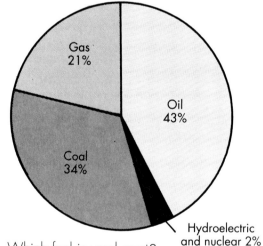

Gas 21%
Oil 43%
Coal 34%
Hydroelectric and nuclear 2%

a) Which fuel is used most?
b) Which of the fuels are fossil fuels?
c) Why are they called fossil fuels?
d) What is done to fossil fuels in order to release their energy?
e) Describe how one non-fossil fuel provides energy.

Science Companions 1 © A Porter, M Wood, T Wood and Stanley Thornes (Publishers) Ltd, 1991

4. On your own copy, fill in the missing spaces in this passage about nuclear energy using the word list below.

atoms	fuel	generators	heat
radiation	radioactive	stable	steam
turbines	uranium		

In a nuclear power station, the metal called _____ is used as a _____.

The small particles in the metal called _____ break up because they are not very _____. Every time they break up energy is given out in the form of _____.

One gram of uranium can give out as much energy as three tonnes of coal.

The heat from the metal is used to boil water into a gas called _____. This turns large fans called _____ which are connected to machines that make electricity. These are called _____.

The disadvantage of using nuclear fuels is the waste they produce. Each small particle that breaks up gives off _____ as well as heat. The waste material of a nuclear power station can be very _____.

a) What kind of energy is stored in uranium?
b) What kind of energy does the power station supply?
c) What other fuels are used to generate electricity?
d) Why are nuclear power stations built near the coast?

Sellafield nuclear power station and reprocessing plant

5. Use your own copy. Can you change COAL into HEAT by altering one letter at a time? Experts should be able to do it in four moves. Each move must make another proper word.

C	O	A	L
H	E	A	T

Try it yourself

Find out how effective the Sun is at heating up water. Clean out a small food tin and fill it with water. Leave it outside on a warm day and see how hot the water gets.

You could try painting cans different colours. Is black the best at absorbing the heat?

When you have found the best colour you could investigate which material would make the best container. Does the water get warmer if plastic is used instead of tin?

What difference does the size of the container make to how hot the water gets?

Science Companions 1 © A Porter, M Wood, T Wood and Stanley Thornes (Publishers) Ltd, 1991

Making use of energy

There are many different kinds of energy, so it is difficult to give a simple explanation of what energy is.

We get energy from the food we eat. When we are ill and do not eat much, we feel weak and do not have much energy.

In our homes fuels we burn give out energy. They give out heat to the room.

Transistor radios need two kinds of energy to work. The electricity to power the circuits inside comes from the battery. The aerial picks up energy from the radio waves sent out by the radio station.

Radio waves are similar to light, which is another form of energy. Apart from the light we can see there are other forms of light that are invisible to our eyes. Ultraviolet light can be used to give a sun tan. Infra-red light is used in remote control devices.

Energy chains

All the energy sources that we use on Earth came first from the Sun. Without the Sun's energy there would be no energy sources on Earth.

For any source of energy, you can trace back where the energy came from. You end up with a **chain** of energy sources, and each energy chain should lead you back to the Sun.

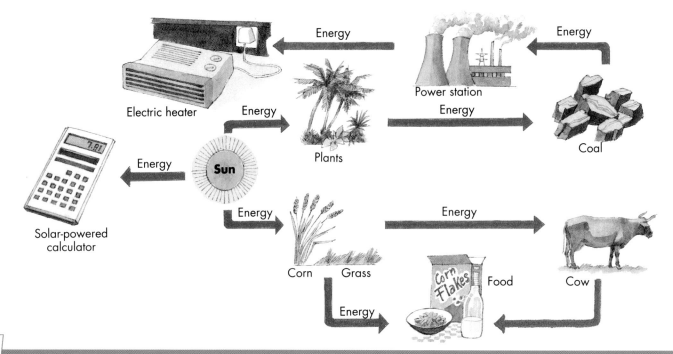

Electric heater — Energy — Plants — Energy — Power station — Energy — Coal

Solar-powered calculator — Energy — Sun — Energy — Corn / Grass — Energy — Cow — Food

Batteries

There are many different kinds of 'battery' on the market today. Most of them are not really batteries – the word 'battery' means a group of **cells**. Most 'batteries' are in fact single cells.

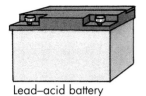
Lead–acid battery

Mercury cell

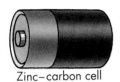
Zinc–carbon cell

Alkaline cell

Nickel–cadmium cell

Different cells provide different amounts of energy depending on their size and what they are made from. Inside all cells is a mixture of chemicals. The chemicals react to produce electricity. **Never try to open any cell** – a lot of the chemicals used are poisonous or corrosive.

Most cells will eventually 'go flat'. That means the chemicals inside are used up and will produce no more electricity. Some cells can be **recharged**. Electricity is put back into the cell. This restores the chemicals and the cell can be re-used. The lead–acid battery in a car and the nickel–cadmium cell are rechargeable. **Never try to recharge a cell that is not clearly labelled 'rechargeable'.**

The energy from a cell is released when we connect it to something that can use it (something that can conduct electricity).

Rubber bands

When you stretch an elastic material, like rubber, you put energy into it. The energy has come from your muscles, which get their energy from the food you eat.

The energy in the stretched rubber band can be used if you let it go.

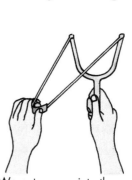
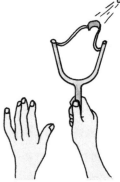

We put energy into the rubber band by stretching it.

The energy is used to move the pellet.

We can also stretch a rubber band by twisting it. This time, releasing the rubber band gives us energy in a turning motion.

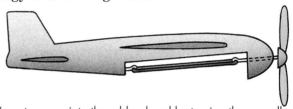

We put energy into the rubber band by turning the propeller. The energy is used to turn the propeller quickly and so move the plane.

QUESTIONS

1. Where do infra-red remote control devices get their energy from?

2. What kinds of food are usually associated with high energy?

3. Make up an energy chain for the petrol used in a car engine.

4. What happens when cells are recharged?

5. What two warnings should you remember about cells and batteries?

6. Name one or more examples of

   a) heat energy
   b) light energy
   c) sound energy
   d) food energy
   e) electrical energy.

1. There are 23 words hidden in the wordsearch. Each one has been mentioned in section 5.1 or 5.2. Write down each word as you find it.

E	U	L	T	R	A	V	I	O	L	E	T
N	U	S	H	N	P	H	C	O	A	L	A
E	K	S	G	S	O	U	N	D	D	E	E
R	A	D	I	O	W	A	V	E	S	C	H
G	Q	L	L	E	C	R	P	D	T	B	
Y	N	P	E	R	R	A	L	O	S	R	C
E	L	I	I	A	R	U	O	I	R	I	I
R	X	A	N	F	D	F	I	S	E	C	T
I	L	M	N	R	U	A	L	O	B	I	S
F	T	I	N	M	U	E	C	N	B	T	A
Y	R	E	T	T	A	B	L	I	U	Y	L
P	R	E	C	H	A	R	G	E	D	F	E

3. Look at the pie chart below. It tells you how much energy an average house gets 'for free'. We normally think of paying to heat our rooms. Fuels and electricity only provide half of the heat our homes get. The figures in the pie chart show you where this other heat comes from.

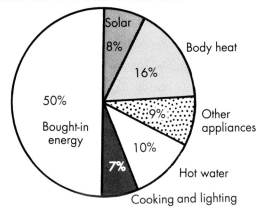

a) Which energy supplies most of this extra heat?
b) What is the source of this heat?
c) Which source of energy comes from outside the house?
d) How could we make more of this particular energy source?
e) Name three small appliances, other than heaters, which would help to warm up a room.
f) Why do lights warm up a room?

2. On your own copy, draw the correct picture from those on the right in each empty box.

Energy change: to ⋯ from	Electrical energy	Heat	Chemical energy
Electrical energy	Pylons		Electrolysis
Heat	Digital thermometer		
Chemical energy			Reactions

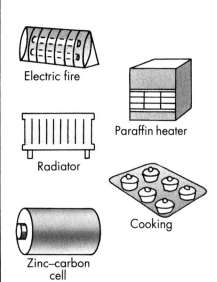

Electric fire

Paraffin heater

Radiator

Cooking

Zinc–carbon cell

Science Companions 1 © A Porter, M Wood, T Wood and Stanley Thornes (Publishers) Ltd, 199

1. Make a list of all the devices which use cells in your house. How many cells do they use? What size are the cells? What voltage do they give out? What are they made from? Copy the headings and complete a table like this.

Device	Number of cells	Size of cells	Voltage of each cell	Total voltage	Type of cell
Torch	3	R20	1.5 V	4.5 V	Zinc–carbon
Walkman	2	MN1500	1.5 V	3 V	Alkaline

2. You can detect the energy that you put into a rubber band when you stretch it. Hold a rubber band loosely between your hands. Put your lips on the rubber band. Now stretch the band. Pause for a while and gently let the rubber band return to normal.

a) What happens when the rubber band is stretched? Do your lips detect anything?
b) What happens when the band returns to normal?
c) How can you explain this?

3. *Cotton reel tank*

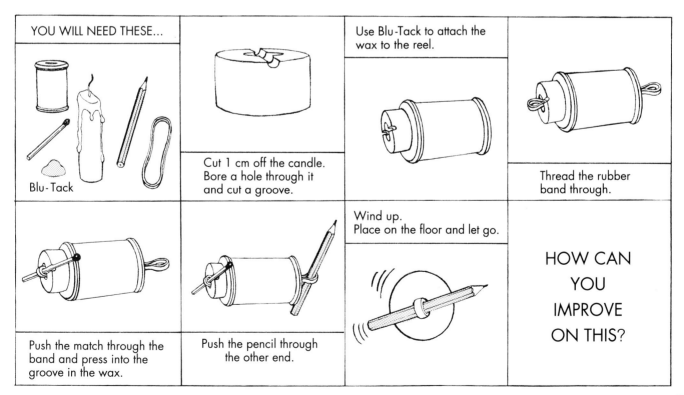

YOU WILL NEED THESE...

Blu-Tack

Cut 1 cm off the candle. Bore a hole through it and cut a groove.

Use Blu-Tack to attach the wax to the reel.

Thread the rubber band through.

Push the match through the band and press into the groove in the wax.

Push the pencil through the other end.

Wind up. Place on the floor and let go.

HOW CAN YOU IMPROVE ON THIS?

Storing energy

We have looked at a number of fuels or energy sources which have energy stored within them. There are many different kinds of stored energy – they are all called **potential energy**. This is because the energy has the potential to be used but it is somehow locked up.

Rubber bands have potential energy stored inside them when they are stretched.

Batteries or cells have electrical energy stored inside them.

Gas and other fossil fuels have chemical energy stored in them.

Under the right conditions the stored energy can be released and used. Then the energy is changed into other forms. One useful form is moving energy, called **kinetic energy**. The word kinetic comes from the same Greek word that gives us cinema – moving pictures.

Making things move

Electricity can be used to power motors. The electrical energy makes a coil of wire turn inside the motor. The coil can be attached to many other devices.

These appliances use an electric motor.

Belts

The electric motor cannot power many things directly. Most devices use one or more **belts** to transfer the motion from the motor to other parts. Belts can be seen on many machines.

The chain on the bicycle can transfer the energy that legs give the pedals to the back wheel.

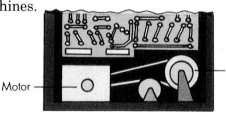

Motor —

— Drive wheel

The belt in a cassette recorder transfers the energy from the motor to the drive wheel.

In a car the fan belt is used to drive several other parts of the car.

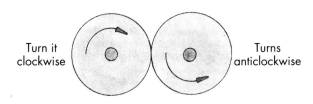

Turn it clockwise

Turns anticlockwise

The turning motion of a motor can be made to power something in the opposite direction. If two wheels are placed side by side, turning one makes the other turn in the opposite direction.

This can be improved by putting teeth on to the wheels. These wheels are called **cogs**.

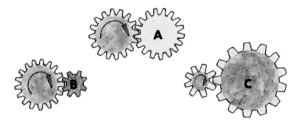

The speed the second cog turns at depends on its size. When the cogs are of different sizes the combination is known as a **gear**.

For one turn of the left-hand cog
- A will turn once in the other direction
- B will turn more than once (i.e. faster)
- C will turn less than once (i.e. slower).

Gears are used to transfer the energy from one cog to another. On a bicycle, the cogs are joined by a chain. One cog is attached to the pedals, the other is attached to the back wheel. On the back wheel there are different sized cogs. The chain can swap between these cogs.

If the back wheel cog is smaller than the pedal cog, the back wheel will turn quickly. This is a high gear, used when going along a flat surface or downhill.

If the back wheel cog is larger, the back wheel will go slower. This is a low gear, used for going uphill.

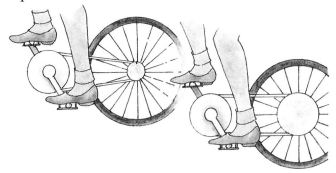

The golf ball machine

QUESTIONS

1. Explain in your own words how the muscle energy of the man turning the handle is used to lift the golf balls out of the hole (see opposite).

2. Explain what is meant by potential energy and kinetic energy.

3. What drives the fan belt in a motor car? What is the fan belt used for?

4. Why does a cyclist choose first gear to go up a steep slope?

1. The drawing below shows you how far you could get for about £2 worth of fuel per person. For the car, this is about one gallon (5 litres) of petrol. It also shows you the number of people you can transport this distance.

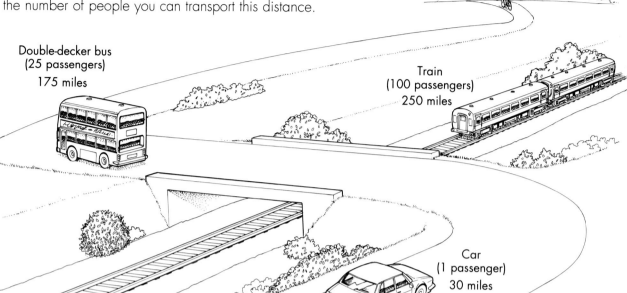

Cycling
1600 miles

Double-decker bus
(25 passengers)
175 miles

Train
(100 passengers)
250 miles

Car
(1 passenger)
30 miles

a) Which form of transport is the most wasteful of fuel?
b) What advantage is there in this form of transport?
c) How might the distance travelled per person be improved?
d) The bus will use almost the same amount of fuel whether it runs full or empty.
What would the distance per person be if there were 50 people on the bus?
e) What fuel do each of the forms of transport use?
f) Which is the cleanest form of transport? Why?

2. Work out whether turning the handle will raise the bucket or lower it further down the well.

3. The following figures show the 1988 prices for four different fuels. Each price is for the same amount of fuel.

Type of fuel	Price for one unit
Coal	16.5p
Fuel oil	13.5p
Gas	22.0p
Electricity	88.0p

a) What is the majority of coal used for in this country?
b) Where does fuel oil come from?
c) For each fuel, give one example showing how it is used to transport things or people.
d) Why do you think electricity is more expensive than the other fuels?

Science Companions 1 © A Porter, M Wood, T Wood and Stanley Thornes (Publishers) Ltd, 1991

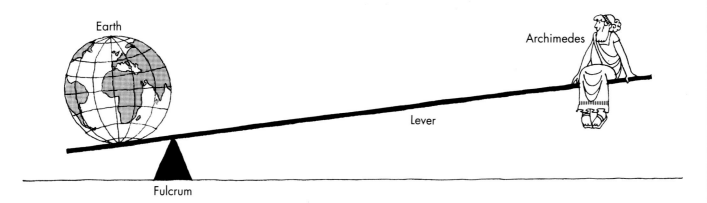

Earth

Archimedes

Lever

Fulcrum

4. *'Give me a place to stand and I can move the world.'*

These are the words of Archimedes who was the first person to understand how levers transfer energy from one place to another. A **lever** works like a see-saw. It is a strong pole which can turn about a fixed point called a **fulcrum**.

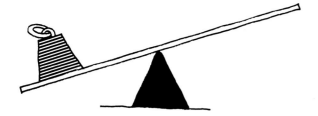

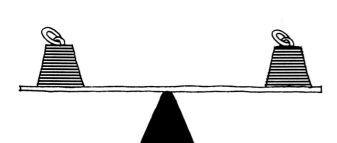

If a heavy weight is placed on one end of the lever, that end drops down. It takes an equally heavy weight on the other end to balance the lever again.

However, if one side of the lever is longer, one weight can be placed further away from the fulcrum. At a greater distance, less force is needed to balance the lever. This is why Archimedes said he could move the world. He realised that with a long enough lever he could move something as heavy as the Earth.

We use much smaller levers to make it easier to move things. Levers help us to use less energy.

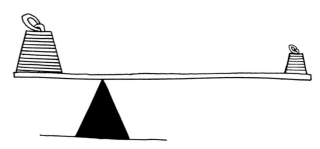

a) What is a lever?
b) What is a fulcrum?
c) What is a crowbar used for? Why is it like a lever?
d) What other objects can you think of that behave like a lever?

Try it yourself

Balance a long ruler over a pencil. Place a pile of coins on one end and push down on the other end until the ruler is level. Now try pushing down half-way between the end of the ruler and the pencil. Is it easier or harder to balance the ruler?

Try pushing in other places along the ruler. What can you say about how easy it is to push at different positions?

Try moving the pile of coins and also the pencil. Does the same thing happen?

Why is it a good idea to have door handles on the edge of the door, far away from the hinges?

Science Companions 1 © A Porter, M Wood, T Wood and Stanley Thornes (Publishers) Ltd, 1991

Energy conservation

James Prescott Joule (1818–89)

Joule was born into a brewing family in Salford near Manchester. When he was young he received his science education from John Dalton, the man responsible for our present ideas about atoms.

Later in life Joule found out that energy was the ability to do work of some kind. This idea makes sense – a person with a lot of energy can do more work than someone with less energy. A fuel that has more energy stored inside it can boil more water than a fuel with less energy. This makes more steam, which can do more work in a steam engine.

By experimenting, Joule found that no matter what work was done, heat was produced.

He thought that heat and work must be the same thing. They were both kinds of energy. Energy can change from heat to work and from work to heat.

In honour of the work Joule did on energy, the units of energy are now called **joules**. The old name, **calories**, is still sometimes used. Here are some examples of how much energy is stored in some fuels, and how much work some appliances do (how fast they use energy).

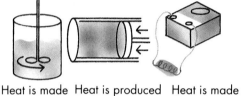

Heat is made when water is stirred   Heat is produced when a gas is squeezed   Heat is made when electricity is used

Whenever work is done, heat is produced, especially when moving parts rub together. If you add up all the heat produced by a device and the work it has done, the total will equal the energy it used. No energy is lost. The energy is just changed into different forms.

Fuels (energy per gram)		Work (joules per hour)	
Coal	30 000 joules	Colour TV	4 million
Methane	55 000 joules	Fan heater	7 million
Wood	17 000 joules	Fridge	300 thousand
Paraffin	48 000 joules		

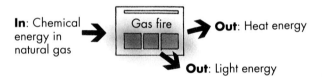

In: Chemical energy in natural gas → Gas fire → **Out**: Heat energy
Out: Light energy

In: Chemical energy in petrol → **Out**: Heat energy
Out: Kinetic energy
Out: Sound energy

Renewable energy sources

We have to use alternatives to fossil fuels wherever it is practical to do so. At the moment scientists are researching new ways of using energy sources that are renewable.

Wind

The energy of the wind has been used for a long time to grind corn in windmills. Now there are many power stations that change wind energy into electrical energy, and many more are planned.

Wind turbines in California

Water provides energy when it moves. Dams can be built to control the flow of water in a river. The water is squeezed through small channels where it turns fans to make electricity. This happens in **hydroelectric power stations**.

The regular motion of waves can also provide energy to generate electricity. There are plans to construct large generators across the mouths of certain rivers so that when the tide comes in the flow of water will produce electricity.

Hoover Dam, Nevada, USA

Geothermal energy

Geothermal power station in Iceland. The bathers are swimming in the waste hot water from the power station, said to be good for health.

In power stations, steam is made by boiling water. The steam is then used to turn fans which makes electricity. At present, fossil fuels provide most of the energy to boil the water.

Instead of using these fuels, it is possible to use the hot rocks that lie under the Earth's crust. Water is forced down long pipes into the Earth, and these rocks heat it. This form of energy is called **geothermal energy** and is used in places such as New Zealand, Iceland and Hawaii. In these places the hot rocks are close to the surface, so the pipes do not have to be very long.

Solar energy

The Sun will provide energy for millions of years to come. More **solar energy** reaches the Earth from the Sun in one hour than is used by the world in one year. However, we are not very good at trapping it and using it.

- We can use solar energy directly to make hot water.
- Houses can be designed so that south-facing windows are large and trap the Sun's heat during the day.
- **Solar cells** change sunlight into electricity. General Motors have built and tested a car that used solar power in this way, though it was very expensive to produce.

QUESTIONS

1. Which of the four fuels listed on the opposite page has the most energy stored inside it?

2. What types of energy are given out by a car?

3. How can the following things provide electrical energy:
   a) wind
   b) water
   c) hot rocks
   d) the Sun?

1. Read this newspaper article and then answer the questions below.

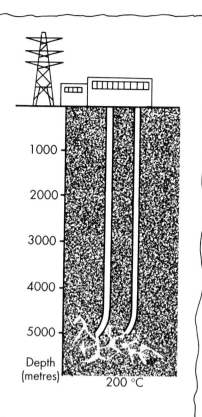

ENERGY NEWS

Hot rocks may heat towns in future

Experiments carried out in Cornwall could lead the way in solving our energy problems.

At the Camborne School of Mines, they have been testing the usefulness of geothermal energy. The energy that forms volcanoes and flows of molten rock is being used to heat up cold water.

Although there are no volcanoes in Cornwall, the rocks below the surface are still hot enough to provide energy to heat the water pumped down there.

Two long holes have been drilled

2000 metres deep into the Earth's crust. A small explosion at the bottom of the pipes has opened up cracks in the rocks. Now cold water can be pumped down one pipe and forced along the cracks in the hot rocks and back up to the surface as hot water.

It is estimated that four such geothermal stations would be needed to supply a town the size of Truro. In other parts of the country holes may have to be drilled much deeper, to 5000 metres.

a) In your own words describe how the water is heated in the geothermal station.

b) How far down are the hot rocks in Cornwall?

c) What uses can you think for the hot water produced in these stations?

d) Why would the holes in similar stations in other parts of the country have to be deeper?

e) Where in the world would the pipes be shorter? Why?

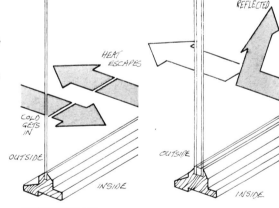

2. Look at these diagrams and answer the questions below.

a) Give two reasons why a single pane of glass is not as good as double glazing.

b) What is the effect of increasing the gap between the panes of glass in double glazing?

c) 20 mm is the best size of gap. Why?

d) What other advantage may double glazing offer?

e) What are the disadvantages of double glazing?

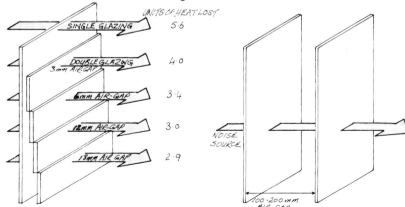

Relative heat losses decrease with increased width of air-gap

Where noise is a problem, considerably greater air-gaps are called for

Science Companions 1 © A Porter, M Wood, T Wood and Stanley Thornes (Publishers) Ltd, 1991

3. a) What does the Manx Electricity Authority do?
   b) What fossil fuel does the authority use?
   c) How many power stations use this fuel?
   d) What other way of generating electricity is there?
   e) What provides the energy for this station?
   f) How is the electricity supplied to the customers?
   g) How many people are supplied with electricity?
   h) What problems do you think the authority might face in getting fuel?

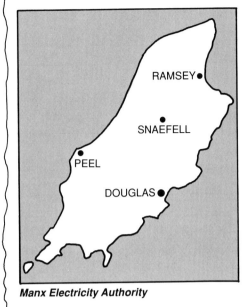

Manx Electricity Authority

Manx Electricity Authority

The Manx Electricity Authority is responsible for the provision and maintenance of a public supply of electricity in the Isle of Man under the terms of the Electricity Act 1984.

The Authority has three diesel generating stations at Douglas, Peel and Ramsey, and also has a small hydroelectric station. The total plant capacity is 97.15 MW.

The Island's population of 70 000 is served by a distribution network of 33 000, 11 000 and 3300 volt cables via approximately 850 substations.

MWh sales are currently approximately 215 000 per year.

Harcroft, Douglas, Isle of Man

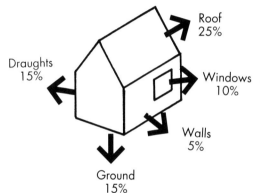

Roof 25%

Draughts 15%

Windows 10%

Walls 5%

Ground 15%

4. The diagram opposite shows how heat escapes from a house. The house is empty, with no insulation, furniture or fittings.

   a) List the five ways that heat escapes from the house. Put them in order from the largest loss to the smallest.
   b) For each of the five ways say what could be done to stop so much heat escaping.

5. Yorkshire Water have built a network of pipes that links all parts of the area. This means that in times of drought, water can be shared out across the region and no area will face severe shortages of water. The scheme requires electricity to run the pumps.

   At the moment the water company buys its electricity from the electricity board, but it plans to build a wind farm similar to the one shown in the photograph. The wind turbines will provide the electricity needed to run the pumps and any extra electricity can be sold to the electricity board. If there is a shortage of wind the water company can buy electricity from the electricity board.

   a) There are more days of windy weather in the winter. Why is this an advantage in the scheme?
   b) Can you think of one disadvantage?
   c) Why might the wind farm be seen as a more environmentally friendly scheme, compared with buying the electricity from the electricity board?
   d) What objections might people have to the wind farm?
   e) What can you say about the price of the electricity bought from the electricity board, compared with that sold to the board from the wind farm?

Science Companions 1 © A Porter, M Wood, T Wood and Stanley Thornes (Publishers) Ltd, 1991

Human life and activity – the energy we need

Humans need energy to live. The fuel we use to give us energy is food. The food we eat is converted into energy by chemical reactions in the body. We use food and oxygen to make the energy which helps us move, breathe, walk, keep warm, and carry out all our bodily functions.

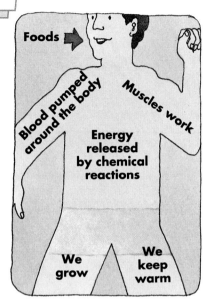

Foods

Blood pumped around the body

Muscles work

Energy released by chemical reactions

We grow

We keep warm

Foods mainly for growth

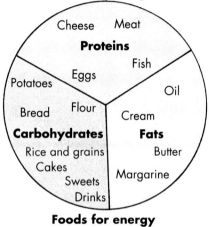

Cheese Meat
Proteins
Fish
Eggs
Potatoes
Oil
Bread Flour
Cream
Carbohydrates **Fats**
Rice and grains Butter
Cakes
Sweets Margarine
Drinks

Foods for energy

The foods we eat belong to different groups and do different jobs. Not all foods give us energy.

Foods which contain mainly sugar and starch are called **carbohydrates**. These are the body's main fuel and give us most of our energy. Foods which contain mainly fat give us more energy per gram than carbohydrates and are useful for storing energy in our bodies.

What are the units of energy?

You will have seen energy values on food packets. They show how many units of energy the food contains. The units used are kilocalories (kcal or Cal) and kilojoules (kJ).

A kilocalorie is the same unit of energy as the Calories used in slimming diets. A kilojoule is the metric unit of energy which must be shown on food labels by law.

One kilocalorie is the same as 4.2 kilojoules. From this biscuit packet, one biscuit gives you 34 kcal.

34 kcal x 4.2 = 142 kJ

NUTRITION INFORMATION		
	TYPICAL COMPOSITION	
	per biscuit	per 100g
	142kJ	1984kJ
ENERGY	34kcal	470kcal
PROTEIN	0.5g	6.7g
CARBOHYDRATE	5.3g	74.2g
FAT	1.1g	15.7g

Rich Tea biscuits

Which foods give you energy?

Some of the foods we eat, especially snacks, are high in energy because they contain a lot of carbohydrate and fat. These figures show the energy for 100 g of each food (roughly one portion).

Chocolate 420 kcal/1764 kJ

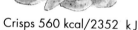

Crisps 560 kcal/2352 kJ

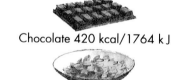

Cereal 400 kcal/1680 kJ

Apple 40 kcal/168 kJ

Lettuce 12 kcal/50 kJ

Fried fish 224 kcal/1740 kJ

Yogurt 100 kcal/420 kJ

Chips 228 kcal/958 kJ

Pasteurised milk 380 kcal/1396 kJ

Cheeseburger (whole) 1200 kcal/5040 kJ

Cheese and onion pasty 1180 kcal/4956 kJ

Butter 840 kcal/3528 kJ

How much energy do we need?

The table shows the amount of energy needed on average by different people each day. Individual people need enough energy for their particular lifestyle.

Person	Energy needed per day (kJ)
Child aged 2	500
Child aged 6	7500
Girl aged 15	9500
Boy aged 15	12 000
Woman doing light work	10 500
Man doing light work	12 200
Woman doing heavy work	12 600
Man doing heavy work	15 200

The amount of energy needed depends on a person's body size, age, sex and activity. Men usually need more energy than women because on average they have a higher body weight than women.

If you do not take in exactly the amount of energy shown in the table each day, there is no need to worry. Your body uses energy from energy stores if you take in fewer kilojoules. But if you regularly take in too much or too little energy you can develop health problems.

Do we need energy all the time?

We need energy for every single activity that we do. When we are asleep, we still need energy to work our bodies, for pumping blood and breathing. When we are more active we use more energy than when we are resting. The chart opposite shows how much energy is needed per minute for each activity, in kilojoules.

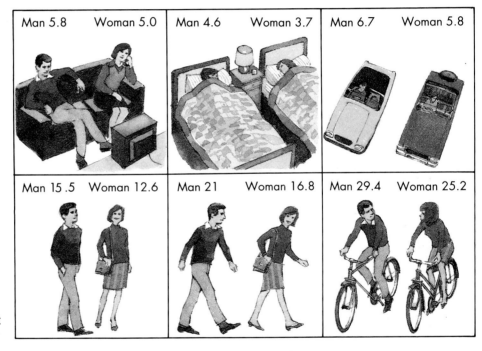

Man 5.8   Woman 5.0   Man 4.6   Woman 3.7   Man 6.7   Woman 5.8
Man 15.5   Woman 12.6   Man 21   Woman 16.8   Man 29.4   Woman 25.2

Energy needed to carry out one minute of each activity

QUESTIONS

1. What fuel do humans need?

2. Which foods give us energy?

3. How is energy stored in our bodies?

4. How can we convert kilocalories to kilojoules?

5. Using the food pictures which show energy per 100 g of food, list the foods in order from highest in energy to lowest.

6. Why do different people need different amounts of food?

7. How much energy, on average, does a 15-year-old boy need per day? How much does a girl of the same age need?

8. Why do we need energy when we are asleep?

9. How many kilojoules does a man use up when watching television for half an hour?

1. Look at this chart of exercises. It shows how many minutes of each exercise you need to do to use 500 kJ of energy.

Exercise	Time
Jogging	19 minutes
Walking briskly	20 minutes
Tennis	24 minutes
Squash	12 minutes
Cycling	16 minutes
Circuit training	10 minutes
Golf	30 minutes
Stretch exercises	40 minutes

a) Draw a block graph to show the results.
b) Which exercise burns up most energy?
c) Which exercise burns up least energy?
d) How many minutes of cycling would a person need to do to use up 1500 kJ of energy?
e) Try to explain why different exercises use up different amounts of energy.

2. Look carefully at the information on each of these food labels, and then answer the questions which follow.
a) Why is information given for 100 g of each product?
b) Why are the energy levels shown in kilocalories and kilojoules?
c) List the products in order from the highest in energy to the lowest.
d) Which product gives the most energy per 100 g of food?
e) Why does this product give most energy?

An average serving of *All-Bran* cereal (40 grammes) supplies 50% of your daily fibre needs. It also provides at least 33% of the recommended daily amount (RDA) of the vitamins niacin, riboflavin, thiamin, folic acid, vitamin D, and vitamin B_{12}; and the mineral iron. *All-Bran* supplies 108 kcal per 40g serving.

NUTRITION INFORMATION

Each Gives You	Bar	100 g
Energy kJ	347	1806
kcal	83	432
Protein	1.1 g	5.6 g
Carbohydrate	13.2 g	68.6 g
Fat	3.2 g	16.9 g
(of which saturates	2.2 g	11.2 g)

INGREDIENTS: MILK CHOCOLATE, GLUCOSE SYRUP, SUGAR, HYDROGENATED VEGETABLE FAT, SKIMMED MILK POWDER, FAT-REDUCED COCOA, WHEY POWDER, MILK FAT, MALT EXTRACT, SALT, EGG WHITE, HYDROLYSED MILK PROTEIN, FLAVOURING.

Milk chocolate contains milk solids 14% minimum, vegetable fat, emulsifier: lecithin and flavouring

INGREDIENTS
WHEAT BRAN, SUGAR, SALT, MALT FLAVOURING, NIACIN, IRON, VITAMIN B_6, RIBOFLAVIN (B_2), THIAMIN (B_1), FOLIC ACID, VITAMIN D, VITAMIN B_{12}.

NUTRITION INFORMATION Per 100g

ENERGY	1150	kJ
	270	kcal
PROTEIN	15	g
CARBOHYDRATE	45	g
of which sugars 19 g		
starch 26 g		
FAT	3.0	g
of which saturates 0.7 g		
SODIUM	0.9	g
FIBRE	24	g
VITAMINS:		
NIACIN	16	mg
VITAMIN B_6	1.8	mg
RIBOFLAVIN (B_2)	1.5	mg
THIAMIN (B_1)	1.0	mg
FOLIC ACID	250	μg
VITAMIN D	2.8	μg
VITAMIN B_{12}	1.7	μg
IRON	12	mg

750 g

Carton No. 14 23 19/49

NUTRITIONAL VALUE

Typical per 100g uncooked.
Energy 335kcal   Carbohydrate 74.6g
Protein 8.2g   Dietary Fibre 3.5g

A satisfying serving of Tilda Rice has around only 70 calories, the equivalent of one digestive biscuit!
(Information based on boiled rice without butter, oil or salt.)

3. The following list shows the food eaten in a day by Jim, a schoolboy. An average schoolboy needs about 12 000 kJ a day. Study the information and then answer the questions which follow.

Food	Energy (kJ)
Cereal	325
Chocolate bar	1134
Sausage and chips	2050
Beans	460
Cake	1350
2 chocolate biscuits	1932
3 Coca-colas	1827
Cream doughnut	735
Pizza	2730

Fact file
- Occupation – schoolboy
- Hobbies – watching TV, video games
- Gets a lift to and from school
- Plays football once a week.

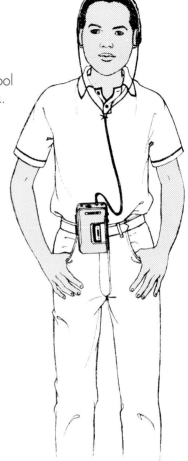

a) Add up Jim's total energy intake for the day in kJ.
b) Comment on Jim's energy intake.
c) What makes Jim's foods high in energy?
d) What could happen if Jim's energy intake stayed at this level?
e) Suggest ways that Jim can reduce his energy intake.
f) How could Jim burn off more energy?
g) What might happen if Jim reduced his energy intake to 7000 kJ a day?

4. Use your own copy. Work out the clues to find the units of energy in the outlined column.

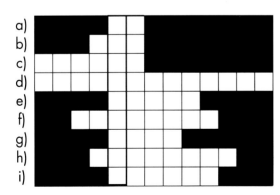

a) Short for a unit of energy.
b) A fat which is high in energy.
c) A small amount.
d) Foods high in energy.
e) A small unit of energy, in full.
f) Foods needed for growing.
g) Energy is _____ up during exercise.
h) You use energy even when you do this.
i) Made from food and oxygen.

Research

Look up energy values on food packets. List the energy values of 15 different kinds of foods. Make two lists, one of high-energy foods and one of low-energy foods.

cience Companions 1 © A Porter, M Wood, T Wood and Stanley Thornes (Publishers) Ltd, 1991

Index